Police, Picket-Lines and Fatalities

Other Palgrave Pivot titles

Lassi Heininen (editor): **Security and Sovereignty in the North Atlantic**

Steve Coulter: **New Labour Policy, Industrial Relations and the Trade Unions**

Ayman A. El-Desouky: **The Intellectual and the People in Egyptian Literature and Culture: Amāra and the 2011 Revolution**

William Van Lear: **The Social Effects of Economic Thinking**

Mark E. Schaefer and John G. Poffenbarger: **The Formation of the BRICS and Its Implication for the United States: Emerging Together**

Donatella Padu: **John Maynard Keynes and the Economy of Trust: The Relevance of the Keynesian Social Thought in a Global Society**

Davinia Thornley: **Cinema, Cross-Cultural Collaboration, and Criticism: Filming on an Uneven Field**

Lou Agosta: **A Rumor of Empathy: Rewriting Empathy in the Context of Philosophy**

Tom Watson: **Middle Eastern and African Perspectives on the Development of Public Relations: Other Voices**

Adebusuyi Isaac Adeniran: **Migration and Regional Integration in West Africa: A Borderless ECOWAS**

Craig A. Cunningham: **Systems Theory for Pragmatic Schooling: Toward Principles of Democratic Education**

David H. Gans and Ilya Shapiro: **Religious Liberties for Corporations?: Hobby Lobby, the Affordable Care Act, and the Constitution**

Samuel Larner: **Forensic Authorship Analysis and the World Wide Web**

Karen Rich: **Interviewing Rape Victims: Practice and Policy Issues in an International Context**

Ulrike M. Vieten (editor): **Revisiting Iris Marionyoung on Normalisation, Inclusion and Democracy**

Fuchaka Waswa, Christine Ruth Saru Kilalo, and Dominic Mwambi Mwasaru: **Sustainable Community Development: Dilemma of Options in Kenya**

Giovanni Barone Adesi (editor): **Simulating Security Returns: A Filtered Historical Simulation Approach**

Daniel Briggs and Dorina Dobre: **Culture and Immigration in Context: An Ethnography of Romanian Migrant Workers in London**

M.J. Toswell: **Borges the Unacknowledged Medievalist**

Anthony Lack: **Martin Heidegger on Technology, Ecology, and the Arts**

palgrave▸pivot

Police, Picket-Lines and Fatalities: Lessons from the Past

David Baker
*Head of Criminal Justice,
Federation University Australia*

© David Baker 2014

All rights reserved. No reproduction, copy or transmission of this publication may be made without written permission.

No portion of this publication may be reproduced, copied or transmitted save with written permission or in accordance with the provisions of the Copyright, Designs and Patents Act 1988, or under the terms of any licence permitting limited copying issued by the Copyright Licensing Agency, Saffron House, 6–10 Kirby Street, London EC1N 8TS.

Any person who does any unauthorized act in relation to this publication may be liable to criminal prosecution and civil claims for damages.

The author has asserted his right to be identified as the author of this work in accordance with the Copyright, Designs and Patents Act 1988.

First published 2014 by
PALGRAVE MACMILLAN

Palgrave Macmillan in the UK is an imprint of Macmillan Publishers Limited, registered in England, company number 785998, of Houndmills, Basingstoke, Hampshire, RG21 6XS.

Palgrave Macmillan in the US is a division of St Martin's Press LLC, 175 Fifth Avenue, New York, NY 10010.

Palgrave Macmillan is the global academic imprint of the above companies and has companies and representatives throughout the world.

Palgrave® and Macmillan® are registered trademarks in the United States, the United Kingdom, Europe and other countries

ISBN: 978-1-137-35807-3 EPUB
ISBN: 978-1-137-35806-6 PDF
ISBN: 978-1-137-35805-9 Hardback

This book is printed on paper suitable for recycling and made from fully managed and sustained forest sources. Logging, pulping and manufacturing processes are expected to conform to the environmental regulations of the country of origin.

A catalogue record for this book is available from the British Library.

A catalog record for this book is available from the Library of Congress.

www.palgrave.com/pivot

DOI: 10.1057/9781137358066

Contents

Preface		vi
List of Abbreviations		viii
1	Police Management of Pickets and Protests: A Global Perspective	1
2	Police and the Marikana Massacre	16
3	Death by Panic: 'Bloody Sunday' on the Fremantle Wharf	36
4	Death by Deliberate Aim: Shootings at Port Melbourne	52
5	Death by Misadventure during the Rothbury Riot	66
6	Lessons for Managing Pickets and Protests	85
Bibliography		94
Index		107

Preface

Police, Picket-lines and Fatalities focuses on some extreme instances of police aggressive and violent behaviour when they were attempting to control industrial disputes. Fatalities have been a rare occurrence in Australian industrial history. There have only been three deaths as a consequence of police confrontations with strikers; these happened in the decade immediately following the Great War. All three happened when police were protecting non-union, strike-breaking labour at worksites. Ruthless actions by police on-the-spot, troubled by some panic and uncertainties, were condoned by police hierarchies, governments and the mainstream press.

If we fast forward to the repressive and brutal Marikana massacre of August 2012 in South Africa, some negative traits emerge of the much earlier Australian fatalities at the hands of police: poorly-trained police, inadequate planning at senior level, and alleged collusion between police and government. For two years the Farlam Commission, itself under some challenge, has been investigating the 44 deaths during the strike-related violence at Marikana. The inquiry's recommendations may indicate whether it has achieved truth and justice for the victims and their families. The coronial inquiries into the three Australian fatalities culminated in a 'whitewash' of police violence collectively and individually.

Above all, this research is about the dynamics of police and worker interaction during protracted and prolonged strikes or lockouts. It is about real people, the people involved in the tragedies – unionists, police, owners, government and local communities. The narratives of these tragedies should be chronicled; they deserve recognition. Hopefully, some crowd management lessons can be extracted from the tragedies in order to avoid some of the violent excesses of the past.

Police, Picket-lines and Fatalities aims to respect the fallen in industrial battles. It does not necessarily condemn the police on-the-spot, who often appeared confused, uncertain and even sometimes manipulated by powerful leaders. The hope is that lessons learnt from such tragedies may prevent any future occurrences of picket-line deaths.

The book is dedicated to the memory of the three fatal victims of police use of force in Australia in the decade after the Great War and to all casualties of the Marikana massacre.

I hope that readers find the book both thought-provoking and valuable.

List of Abbreviations

ACPO	Association of Chief Police Officers
ACTU	Australian Council of Trade Unions
ALF	Australian Labour Federation
AMCU	Association of Mineworkers and Construction Union
ANC	African National Congress
APEC	Asia-Pacific Economic Corporation
APPM	Associated Pulp and Paper Mill
AWU	Australian Workers' Union
MLA	Member of Legislative Assembly
MUA	Maritime Union of Australia
NMH&MA	*Newcastle Morning Herald & Miners' Advocate*
NUM	National Union of Miners
PPUs	police paramilitary units
SABC	South African Broadcasting Corporation
SAP	South African Police
SAPS	South African Police Service
SMH	*Sydney Morning Herald*

1
Police Management of Pickets and Protests: A Global Perspective

Abstract: *The policing of industrial pickets and demonstrations is unpredictable, volatile and problematic. The public order literature indicates that policing in the Western world has generally experienced trends from 'escalated force' to 'negotiated management' to 'strategic incapacitation' in the monitoring and controlling of large-scale dissent. Historically in Australia, police ruthlessly, and sometimes brutally, quelled hostile industrial unrest. Three worker fatalities at the hands of police in early Australia form the centrepiece of this book. In August 2012, the South African Police Service shot dead 34 striking miners at Marikana. The Australian fatalities and those at modern-day Marikana are extreme and exceptional examples of police use of lethal force, but they convey important narratives and significant lessons for the policing of pickets and protests.*

Keywords: Australia; fatalities; Marikana; police; protests; strikes

Baker, David. *Police, Picket-Lines and Fatalities: Lessons from the Past.* Basingstoke: Palgrave Macmillan, 2014. DOI: 10.1057/9781137358066.0004.

State and police control

Public order policing, in particular the policing of protest, is increasingly complex, uncertain and vexatious. The art of policing is selective, especially so in maintaining public order. Large-scale protests and picketing represent considerable challenges for police in attempting to balance safety and security with the civil rights of its citizens. As regulatory agents, police encounter this perennial dilemma of how to reconcile people's rights to express grievance while maintaining the policing mandate of order and security. Throughout industrial history, police capacity to make sound, strategic choices when handling overt manifestations of industrial disputation – pickets and lockouts – has tested police doctrines of independence and impartiality and challenged police organizational skills, resources and tactics.

Police legitimacy is entwined with the broader legitimacy and acceptance of the state. The hegemony of the state is entrusted to the police force which possesses the monopoly to use coercion. This power authorized by the power elite reflects Antonio Gramsci's theoretical underpinnings of hegemony, the power elite in control of society (Hoare & Smith, 1971, pp. 57–59). Collins (2008, p. 112) argues that the state claims a monopoly on violence, while others are 'expected to keep the peace'. According to Earl (2006, p. 133), 'states have an interest in repressing targets, in part as a demonstration of the state's power'. Demonstrations and pickets may challenge the ruling elite's economic and industrial structure; such conflict threatens police insistence on an orderly 'patch'. O'Malley (1983, p. 56) coined the term 'hegemonic police' to describe a police organization 'not merely as a law enforcement agency but also and especially as an agency of the community, which supplies a broad range of services to secure social order and harmony'. In a democracy, policing services are depicted as being impartially administered, but the police remain the latent coercive arm of state control with 'the capacity for paramilitary, coercive enforcement as the situation demands' (O'Malley, 1983, p. 71).

The police mandate to preserve law and order and protect life and property is tested by street protest if it is perceived as a challenge to police and societal authority. Policing by its nature is conservative and concerned with maintaining the status quo. Police prefer order and predictability on the streets and they expect to win all public disorder confrontations. A large protest or picket presents an affront to the orderly street mentality; it represents an undisciplined situation, a potential problem for 'street cleaning'. Police, with a highly visible street presence, are expected to maintain social control; unruly and riotous behaviour raises questions about police legitimacy and capability.

Police employ discretionary judgements about the use of force, riot squads and weaponry. They determine the parameters of acceptable and unacceptable crowd behaviour, the boundaries of freedom of dissent on the street. Pragmatically, police may claim to facilitate protest, but their coercive powers remain latent to halt the escalation of conflict. Union and protest organizers are conscious of this potential police capacity to use force. The police are in a unique position in society as they are officially licensed to exercise coercion over citizens, but in liberal democracies they are usually able to compel compliance through persuasion, negotiation, compromise or manipulation (Reiner, 2000, pp. 3, 6). The nexus between police and protesters is contentious and unpredictable: no matter how much communication may take place, both sides usually remain somewhat suspicious and distrustful of the motives of the other.

The law in relation to peaceful and passive picketing, an industrial tactic directed at disrupting work and publicising the picketers' demands, is unclear, uncertain and ambiguous (Nyland & Svensen, 1995). Laws in Australia have tended to protect the rights of those with property and business historically at the expense of the working class. If police enforce the letter of the law, this assists commercial enterprises to conduct business unhindered. Police are obliged neither to protect a business interest at any cost nor to placate people's right to protest at any cost. Judicial decisions in Australia have generally supported the legal view that picketing impedes and constrains business unfairly (see Baker, 2001a). The law is also inclined to subordinate political freedoms and civil rights to the demands for law and order and public safety.

Police possess the legitimate capacity to use coercion in public order situations, 'minimum force' appropriate to the circumstances. In practice, decisive police actions in industrial disputes – arrests, physical confrontations, summonses, dislocation of picketers – are directed against workers, especially the union organizers. Police are the controlling and coercive agents of the state; their legitimacy depends on their capacity to maintain public order without losing the consent and compliance of the people. According to P. A. J. Waddington (1994, pp. 101–127), police, as the authority figures, have an obligation to the state to remain in control of public order, including industrial disputes. But, as such, they are bound by the law and the rules of criminal procedures. The exercise of coercive powers must be capable of justification. The police order maintenance role is less clear, less supported and legally and morally ambiguous when compared to the police's traditional crime fighting role of pursuit of criminals. Force, when applied, must be lawful, reasonable and effective (Reiner, 2000, p. 7). Ironically, police determination to win all public battles, especially those with protesting unionists, can lead to a loss of community understanding and support (Baker, 2005).

Police have shown a strong aversion to the disruptiveness inherent in politically illegitimate protest activity and suppressed it accordingly (Vitale, 2007, pp. 404, 406). Advocates of radical social change (peasant revolts, suffragettes, civil rights campaigners, anti-apartheid demonstrators) have historically encountered police opposition. The democratic state is usually restrained in using force against its citizens, but much less restraint is in evidence against those who are marginalized (for instance, the homeless, the powerless, the unemployed, the deprived, militant workers, anarchical radicals, indigenous groups) (White & Perrone, 2005). Groups who are excluded and who do not play by society's rules (for example, 'wildcat' strikers) are prone to police coercion. However, when accessing police policies, one must not forget that in countries like the United Kingdom or Australia, most demonstrations remain non-violent and non-confrontational (Douglas, 2004, p. 104).

A historical perspective

Historically, the baton was the symbol of police public order might. It was the main coercive instrument of crowd dispersal and potentially a source of escalating violence (della Porta & Reiter, 1998, p. 2). In Australia, police with batons, escorting strike-breakers to the workplace was the catalyst that inflamed violent confrontation between unionists and police on the wharves, mines and shearing-sheds. Often police anticipation of major trouble resulted in the fulfilment of that expectation (D. Waddington, 1992, pp. 17–18). When political and ideological clashes between capital and labour were rife amidst the communist hysteria of the 1920s, police saw themselves as defenders of freedom and enforcers of legitimate power, particularly against waterside workers and coal miners (Baker, 2001b). Unemployment rallies and protests of the 1930s were ruthlessly suppressed at the order of police commanders. Radical strikers have often spurned police intervention in industrial confrontation as evidence of collusion between police and employer and government. Skolnick (1971, p. 59) argued that police in industrial disputation were 'necessarily pushed on the side of property' as they perceived 'the striking and sometimes angry workers as their enemy'. Unionists have perceived police as the agent making it possible for the employer to safeguard production by the use of 'blacklegs' or 'scab' labour, the enemy of the unionized workforce.

Historically, police during bitter industrial strife have not been in the middle, as neutral arbiters of the law, but in accord with employer and/or government demands for decisive police action. Employers customarily relied on the apparatus of the state in the form of the police to make their plants accessible, to protect staff and strike-breakers, and to safeguard business productivity. Police have not supported strikers involved in industrial action: police allegiance has been to the state, their employer. Michael Brogden's sociological research (1991, pp. 155–160) of Liverpool police between the two wars highlights the paradoxical position of police who were recruited from lower-class origins in order to perform the instructions of their so-called betters by imposing social order and regulation.

The history of the policing of industrial disputes in Australia covers a motley and erratic pattern of intermittent violence and suppression. Police tactics employed during the processes of curtailing public disorder often provoked considerable criticism rather than the actual police involvement itself. As the coercive arm and guardian of the state, police historically quelled vexatious and hostile industrial unrest (Baker, 2005, pp. 38–43, 53–55). The one rapid and effective method of demolishing a picket-line was for police to smash through it, which appeased employer demands but inflamed hostility between police and picketers. Police perceived picketers, especially ringleaders, as 'trouble', which justified selective and forceful police actions of dispersion and arrest, thereby intensifying and aggravating the unionists' perception that they lived in an unfair and uncaring society.

The police response to industrial mayhem and open challenge by strikers was legalistic and forceful; law and order must be maintained at all costs. Perpetrators of offences were arrested; their obstruction to order and passage suppressed. Disorder was seen as stemming from the actions and provocations of radical extremists (Baker, 2005, pp. 28–49). Police sought to restore normalcy; their view of a stable and controlled public order. The police leadership of the 1920s and 1930s mirrored the hard-line conservative and reactionary position of governments and much of the mainstream press that were consistently anti-communist, anti-unionist and even anti-worker.

The failure of governments to hold police accountable for alleged excesses and violence while controlling industrial and political protest has been a feature of early Australian history. Three workers (Tommy Edwards 1919, Allan Whittaker 1928 and Norman Brown 1929) were killed as the result of frenzied police actions at industrial protests, but no one was ever held to account for the deaths (Baker, 2005, pp. 38–42). These events are the subjects of Chapters 3–5 of this book. Governments, like the police department, refused to investigate these shootings; the coronial inquests merely condoned police action in firing into the surging crowds. The daily press supported police actions – a common scenario of conservative press hostility to industrial unrest. If the triumvirate of government, press and police hierarchies remained steadfast in protecting allegedly excessive police actions, public order policing strategies continued unchecked, constant and unchanged.

The Vietnam War moratoriums and anti-conscription rallies of the late 1960s and early 1970s heralded a major transformation in the policing of mass protest. The limitations of aggressive and repressive police coercion became apparent and gradually new policing approaches were adopted to control protest in Australia. The highly political protests of the 1970s – Vietnam, anti-Springbok, feminist movement activities – were the catalysts for major changes in public order policing when police regularly found themselves outnumbered by street marchers. The introduction of mobile television cameras made both police and protesters more sensitive to the adverse publicity that violence could create. Today, the ubiquitous presence of mobile phone cameras makes visible the public actions of both police and demonstrators. The mere presence of journalists at public events and rallies in some countries appears to tame police 'toughness' (della Porta & Reiter, 1998, p. 18). Union community assemblies, embellished by women and children, appear often to have the same effect (Baker, 1999b). The increasing sophistication of public order planning and training has emerged from reforms instigated by better-educated, management-trained and media-savvy police leaders with greater knowledge of civil rights (Ray Whitrod, S. I. Miller and John Avery are three Australian examples). The creation of police internal investigation units and the advent of civilian oversight agencies have enhanced the accountability of police and hence the progress of police-protester communications.

The literature of the policing of protests: contemporary trends and patterns

The public order literature – McPhail, Schweingruber and McCarthy (1998), della Porta and Reiter (1998), della Porta, Peterson and Reiter (2006), P. A. J. Waddington (2001, 2007), Earl (2003), Earl & Soule (2006), D. Waddington (2007), Vitale (2007), DeMichele (2008), Gorringe, Rosie, Waddington and Kominou (2012) – discusses how the 'escalated force' model of the 1960s of police repressing protest symbolically reinforced state sovereignty, but was flawed by the severe and extreme police responses to protest events (Earl, Soule & McCarthy, 2003, p. 582). This model was superseded by the 'negotiated management' model of the 1990s, which entails a general respect for the right to protest, ongoing communication, regular under-enforcement of the law, force used only as a last resort, and open lines of ongoing communication between police and protesters. McPhail, et al., (1998) argue that the 'negotiated management' model constitutes an effective strategy for police to avoid public order trouble. This strategy has been effective in countries such as Canada and Australia where picket captains have 'policed' and maintained control of members even during agitated industrial disputation (Hall & de Lint, 2003; Baker, 2005). During protest events, police in fact may utilize dialogue and communication skills without awareness of these tactics and their positive impact on crowd behaviour (Hoggett & Stott, 2010, p. 233). This strategy is a means of winning over protest organizers so that they will 'police' themselves. Such a strategy was effective in maintaining peace during the bitter and protracted 1998 Australian waterfront dispute (Baker, 2005, pp. 163–190).

According to Kratcoski, Verma and Das (2001), policing of protest became less violent over the last quarter of the 20th century. della Porta and Reiter (1998, p. 2) contend that in Western democratic countries, many of which historically have been noted for militarized and armed policing (brutal, repressive, confrontational and rigid), there was a widespread trend towards softer, more tolerant, flexible, preventive, selective and less coercive styles of policing protest. Formalized negotiated management between police leaders and protest organizers has lessened the extent of coercive policing intervention through an emphasis on peacekeeping rather than rigid law enforcement. Policing protest in the 1990s was regularly characterized by under-enforcement of the law, the complex procedures of negotiation and the large-scale collection and sharing of prevention-oriented information and intelligence (P. A. J. Waddington, 1999, 2001). The policing of protest seeks containment through negotiation and cooperation with protesters, rather than physical confrontation.

Canadians Hall and de Lint (2003, p. 224) describe 'policing at a distance' when protest organizers monitor and control their own group. Hall and de Lint (2004, p. 360) depict how police in negotiations adroitly communicate the law and lessons of self-regulation to union organizers as 'the substance of communication is to shift the onus of security onto the parties themselves'. Police inform protest organizers of their legal liabilities and responsibilities, which can be a daunting revelation for some. Union picketers have a specific agenda and an immediate identification with the local workplace, colleagues and union history. Hall and de Lint's research (2003, p. 223) indicates a major shift to 'liaison approach policing' of labour disputes in the 1990s. Police can play a pacifying role behind the scenes; set the ground rules of appropriate behaviour; and even delay taking decisive action in order to give the protagonists or the courts time to settle the dispute. But if police are called to a dispute, either major or minor, they implement control and determine what is acceptable and unacceptable picketing behaviour. In recent decades, the relationship between police and unions in Australia has been evolving from hostile confrontation to greater contingency planning, negotiation and accommodation. No longer do employer demands for police action against picketers meet immediate adherence as often happened between the two world wars (Baker, 2007a).

As Gillham and Noakes (2007) assert, limitations have always existed to negotiated management between protesters and police. Such shortcomings can exist in police-unionist encounters, but they are especially evident in contemporary mass anti-globalization protests when police face a hazardous, unpredictable and challenging task when attempting to liaise with diverse, unrepresentative and unstructured masses of people, many of whom have rejected the hierarchical structure. Such denunciation is an anathema to police agencies with their graded ranks and strict chain of command. Also, police do not always adhere to negotiated agreements with protest groups. Ericson and Doyle (1999) detail how the Royal Canadian Mounted Police in 1997 reneged on a negotiated accord with student protesters prior to the Asia-Pacific Economic Cooperation summit at the University of British Columbia. Police, employing preventive arrests, censorship and violent dispersion, rejected protest rights of political expression in favour of 'security concerns'. New Zealand, noted for its liberal democratic approach, witnessed its national police force renege on a series of arrangements with 'Free Tibet' protesters during Chinese President Jiang Zemin's visit in September 1999. New Zealand Police aided Chinese officials by using buses and sirens to obstruct noisy protesters (chanting, singing, whistling and drumming) and Tibetan flags and placards from Zemin's hearing and sight (Baker 2007b).

Much public order policing controversy and reform in Britain has been a response to industrial disputation (1926 general strike, 1972 Saltley, Grunwick 1977, 1984–1985 miners' strike, 1987 Wapping dispute) and soccer hooliganism (Geary, 1985; D. Waddington, 2007). The Association of Chief Police Officers' *Manual of Guidance for Public Order* evolved from the 1980s onwards during periods of industrial dissent, racial riots and football hooliganism in particular. Unions today often contain intelligent and articulate members who are capable of demanding interaction with police leaders (a far cry from football hooligans). Willis (2001, pp. 15–26) argues, from a UK perspective, that policing dissent in general has become less adversarial and more rights-based; in fact, policing is increasingly guaranteeing freedom of expression rather than crushing dissent. This may be true for specific single-issue protests – live animal export blockades, anti-road protests, anti-logging campaigns – but certainly does not apply to the policing of the diverse anti-globalization, anti-capitalism and anti-war protests that have intensified in the new millennium. In the second edition of *The Politics of the Police* (1997, p. 2), Reiner aptly summarized the dual-edged paradox that had emerged in policing public order in Britain: 'Since the mid-80s both the practice and the perception of public order policing has moved to a pragmatic yet brittle acceptance of a style with a greater coercive potential.'

When large numbers are gathered in protest or blockade, police are unable to move and arrest all people who are technically breaking a law. The prudent police approach is often to forego arrests (or pursue a minimum arrest policy) and to preserve the peace. Police remain dominant because the 'soft' response of police is based on the compliance of demonstrators. Contemporary violent confrontation with police is generally a no-win situation for demonstrators because police can utilize their resources, mobility and riot technology if they envisage the situation as demanding it. Almost invariably, confrontations are weighted in favour of police with their modern armoury of stun guns, rubber bullets, tear gas, chemical sprays, riot shields and helmets, horses, dogs, water cannon and armoured personnel carriers. Video surveillance allows police to make arrests at a later stage and not reduce crowd control numbers (Marx, 1998, p. 259). Victoria Police used this arrest strategy extensively after the violent G20 protest in Melbourne in November 2006 (Baker, 2008). Police in Western democracies often communicate a 'carrot and stick' message to protesters that police prefer a low-key approach to controlling demonstrations, but that they are prepared to enforce the law and use force whenever negotiations are breached.

Contemporaneous to 'softer' policing, police have increasingly procured riot weaponry and trained and resourced specialized, paramilitary units. In the 'age of terrorism', police in the Western world have received increased powers; riot technology has become more sophisticated and available; and paramilitary riot and response squads are prevalent. Research in many countries indicates the proliferation and the increasing use of police paramilitary units (PPUs) and special weapons and tactical teams (SWATs) (Kraska and Kappeler 1997 and 2005 for American research; Jefferson 1990 for Britain; McCulloch 2001 for Australia). Kraska and Kappeler (2005) reveal not only the increasing mobilization of PPUs for mainstream and routine aspects of police work, including patrol work, but also the growing direct links between PPUs and the military. When economic and trade interests are at stake, policing has tended to be openly coercive. Riot units have been deployed at union protests and counter-summits in Europe; police have actively discouraged protests (della Porta, et al., 2006, pp. 7–10, 179).

Despite considerable militaristic capabilities, it is pertinent to note that in some countries such as Australia, riot personnel and technology have only been deployed on a limited basis to date. Yet such weaponry exists, it is available if required, and protest leaders and union organizers are well aware of this coercive potential (Baker, 2008). Although there have arguably been notable successes with the negotiated management approach adopted by police, there are signs that policing often involves a two-edged approach of both negotiation with protest leaders and extensive paramilitary preparations based on worst-case scenarios.

There is agreement in the literature that negotiated management has significantly decreased the number and intensity of street clashes between police and demonstrators (Gillham & Noakes, 2007, p. 342). The challenge for police has become how to make negotiation and other violence minimization strategies effective when dealing with diffuse, disorganized and potentially violence-prone protesters. Anti-globalization protests at the turning of the millennium (Davos, Seattle, Melbourne, Gothenburg, Genoa, Washington, Prague, and Quebec) have highlighted the global problems of maintaining public order. The economic trade summits have witnessed the re-emergence of full-scale paramilitary policing reliant upon riot technology, but with only limited success in maintaining order (della Porta, Peterson & Reiter 2006, p. 183). della Porta, et al. (2006) present a compelling case that in the new millennium there has been a reversion to tougher and more brutal policing of large-scale, transnational protests across Europe. Police generally have shown an inclination to use force, construct no-go areas, discourage presence at protests by tactics of warnings and threats of violence, utilize riot technology and accumulate extensive intelligence of demonstrators. This harder edge to policing protest, especially against anti-globalization groups that are perceived as threats to the political elites and governments, has re-ignited confrontation between police and such protesters. Fernandez (2008, p. 4) describes increased fear of violence and police unwillingness to allow protest of any description as a consequence of 9/11. State authorities, led by the police, plan for the 'worst case scenario' in order to suppress diverse, fragmented and unstructured protest, yet those plans can also be deployed against strikers, especially during an unauthorized 'wildcat' strike (Waddington, 2001, pp. 3–14). della Porta, Peterson and Reiter (2006, p. 12) argue that protest rights have receded into the background in the 21st century and that police 'control and command', based on the enforcement of pre-arrest strategies and exclusionary zones, are paramount.

After the 1999 battle of Seattle, Gillham and Noakes (2007, p. 343) who portray a repressive American policing of protest, coined the phrase 'strategic incapacitation' to depict policing that implements obstacles to protest participation and that is characterized by extensive no-protest zones, availability of less-lethal weapons, strategic use of arrests and heavy surveillance. After the 2001 Genoa and Gothenburg summits, authorities have employed rapid forceful responses. The policing of APEC in Sydney, Australia, in early September 2007, is an example of police utilization of exclusionary tactics in a less violent setting than many of the European and American counter summit confrontations (Baker, 2008). Numerous contemporary reports argue that policing of public order has become more heavy-handed in recent years (Joint Committee on Human Rights, 2009). Since 9/11, the Bali bombings, the British underground rail system attack, the Madrid train bombings, numerous suicide bombings in

Pakistan and India and other terrorist attacks, the pendulum has swung back towards a harsher climate of policing dissent in order to protect national security. The widespread show of force by police is interpreted as a tactic of intimidation against would-be protesters, especially those depicted as 'bad'.

Historically, superior numbers were often regarded as the key to police victory over demonstrators. Police, before they decided whether or not to engage in dialogue with protesters, were often influenced by experience and labelling perceptions of whether protesters were 'good' or 'bad' (della Porta, et al., 2006; D. Waddington, 2007). Intelligence, covert surveillance, riot technology and the threat of coercion are the contemporary weapons of police dominance. The public police, the coercive agency of the state, feel obliged to control threatening activities or groups 'without appearing weak to the public' (Earl, Soule & McCarthy, 2003, p. 586). Police encountering protest events believe that they must 'win' the situation in order to maintain control and authority; loss of control would indicate failure and undermine authority for future public order contests (Earl & Soule 2006, pp. 146, 149; Earl, 2006, p. 133).

The study

The Western world has a chequered history of police handling of large-scale protest, including pickets. For much of the 20th century, the police approach involved large police presence to act decisively with force to disperse crowds of protesters (Lovell, 2009, p. 109). Instances of clashes between police and strikers have been fewer in Australia than in France, Britain or the USA, but this negates neither the significance of the violence nor the police function in suppressing union unrest (D. Waddington, 1992, pp. 107–111).

The USA has a bloody history of violent confrontations between police and strikers, including privately-employed police. Taft and Ross (1969), who claim that America has experienced the 'most frequent and bloody labour violence' of any industrial nation, argue that violence in American labour-management relations was pervasive from the 1870s to the 1930s but that this has been less frequent since World War II, apart from the major coal-mining strikes of 1977 and 1981. They ponder the paradox that violence in labour disputes persisted even though it seldom achieved fruitful results. Thiebolt and Haggard (1983, pp.

30–31) present violence as an intricate and traditional part of American labour disputes. Brecher (1997, p. 1) chronicles a pessimistic account of repeated and bloody repression of American worker dissent 'by company-sponsored violence, local police, state militias and the US Army and National Guard'. Despite the precarious and unpredictable nature of the policing of picket-lines, deaths by police have happened rarely in Australia's industrial history, but in the USA it is estimated to be in excess of 700.

This book explores and analyses three case studies in which workers were killed during industrial disputation as the result of the use of police force, the only occasions when such fatalities have resulted in Australia. The three were each innocent victims of conflicts in which they were subjected to police operations. The three are perceived as martyrs to the union cause; the three have become part of labour mythology. These case studies focus on the policing that led to the deaths, the lack of accountability of the police actions and the deficiencies in the administration of justice. The deaths raise the criminological question: were the police merely performing their duty by enforcing the law or were they agents complicit in extreme and reckless repression of workers?

The year 1929 was the last in which a fatal police shooting, the result of a ricocheted bullet, happened during industrial ferment in Australia. A couple of weeks prior to the beginnings of the 1998 national waterfront dispute, Victoria Police Chief Commissioner, Neil Comrie, proclaimed that the volatility and unpredictability of the industrial confrontation created police apprehension of 'serious injury and even loss of life to a number of people' (Terry Laidler program, 17 March 1999; Baker, 2005, p. 163). Negotiated arrangements between senior police and the union movement organizers, backed by community assemblies of workers and families, played a significant role in preventing the 'War on the Wharves', predicted by much of the mainstream media. Due to established police and union protocols and procedures, the industrial conflict failed to culminate in full-scale pitched battle between picketers and the police (Baker, 2005).

Unfortunately and tragically, deaths on picket-lines at the hands of authorities do still occur in some countries. South Africa, Bangladesh and Cambodia are three notorious contemporary examples. In totalitarian regimes, strikes have been viewed as a threat to a state's ruling elites and have been ruthlessly suppressed. In the mid-1980s, under the apartheid regime, the South African Police regularly confronted striking militants who encountered CS smoke or birdshot or ultimately high-velocity rifles if they failed to disperse.

A prolonged and protracted garment workers' dispute from May 2013 led to a series of conflicts in Bangladesh. On 5 June 2013, police fired guns into the air, fired tear gas and then charged protesters with batons, injuring 50. On 18 November 2013, in Ashulia and Gazipur industrial zones, two protesting workers were killed by police; and others received bullet wounds. Thousands demonstrated in response to the police outrage with workers closing more than 200 factories. The Hasina government responded by mobilizing security forces in the country's industrial zones. Police were perceived by many inside and outside the country as an arm of the government (Kumara, 2013). Ultimately industrial disputes are settled: some striking Bangladeshi garment workers in November 2013 won a 77 per cent pay rise to the minimum wage, although it is still the lowest minimum wage in the world.

Three months into a workers' strike, Cambodian riot police shot dead a woman and wounded nine other people on 12 November 2013. About 600 workers were striking about low pay and poor working conditions at the SL Garment factory. Authorities claim that 47 police officers were injured and police vehicles torched in the violent clashes between police and demonstrators. Some protesters hurled rocks and bricks at police who retaliated with water cannons. A wave of clashes escalated into 'hundreds of military police officers' using 38-mm rubber baton rounds, tear gas, live ammunition and shooting with AK-47s and handguns. Eng Sokhum, an innocent 49-year-old bystander who was selling rice inside her shop, died from a bullet wound to the chest. Her daughter lamented: 'There is no use filing a complaint with police ... [they even] threatened me and accused me of being a demonstrator'. The calls for investigation into the excessive use of force and live ammunition and review of arrests of 29 civilians and 12 monks went unheeded (Lipes, 2013). Police intended to conduct their own internal investigation into the civilian shootings, a ploy that human rights advocates, demanding an independent investigation into the series of violent police clashes, believed would result in impunity and no one held accountable (Crothers & Ana, 2013). Police denied culpability in the shooting death as government and police depicted Eng Sokhum's death as collateral damage.

Reminiscent of some apartheid-era police shootings of protesters, police on 16 August 2012 fired at platinum miners engaged in a 'wildcat' strike for higher wages in Marikana, South Africa. The massacre of the

34 miners indicates that death of demonstrating workers from aggressive police actions is not confined to historical events. Although the three Australian fatalities occurred between the two world wars, some universal and contemporary lessons can be drawn from such tragic events. Investigation of the policing of Marikana and the three Australian fatalities provides insights into police rationale of the handling and control of industrial disputes, the inadequate accountability and the subsequent 'cover-ups' of the use of excessive force. The fact that there have been no re-occurrences of police-inflicted striker fatalities in Australia testifies to improvements in the public order policing approach and liaison with the union movement in recent decades.

I must stress that Marikana and the three police fatalities of Australian workers are nine decades apart; the magnitude, locations, contexts and eras are vastly different. The three Australian deaths transpired during different confrontations in the decade after the Great War; the 34 deaths at Marikana occurred in a bloody fury of three minutes. Nevertheless, police agencies and authorities, both historically and contemporaneously, encounter some challenges and problems of public order that remain universal. Policing of pickets and worker demonstrations are precarious and challenging tasks: the dynamics of the physical police-crowd interaction at close personal proximity are fundamental to the encounter. This book is not about comparisons of policing of the two eras (though some do emerge), but rather its focus is the impact and significance of the policing of public order and the lessons to be learnt in order to mitigate the chances of violent confrontations. The case studies are extreme, and exceptional, examples of police use of deadly force but they do highlight what is needed to prevent such tragedies.

2
Police and the Marikana Massacre

Abstract: *On 16 August 2012, police shot dead 34 miners at Marikana, South Africa. This brutal event recalled memories of the 1960 Sharpeville massacre during the apartheid regime. The ill-trained, poorly-led and remilitarized South African Police Service (SAPS) resorted to lethal force to disarm and disperse the miners in order to appease pressures from the government, owners and a rival union to end the 'wildcat' strike. Lack of leadership, faulty equipment and inadequate communication lines added to police problems. The Marikana massacre has tarnished the reputation of SAPS which requires significant cultural and attitudinal reform to transform its public order operations. The Farlam Commission, operating for two years but itself under challenge, is investigating the accountability of protagonists in the massacre, especially the police role.*

Keywords: Farlam Commission; Lonmin; Marikana massacre; South African Police Service; violence; 'wildcat' strike

Baker, David. *Police, Picket-Lines and Fatalities: Lessons from the Past.* Basingstoke: Palgrave Macmillan, 2014. DOI: 10.1057/9781137358066.0005.

Most industrial disputes are resolved without police involvement. When police are employed to control industrial protest and picketing, they often do so without the resort to force, especially lethal force. Deliberately, the cases selected for this book are extremes, worst case scenarios. These severe and excessive cases highlight violence and disorder; they provide lessons for improved police practice in order to avoid future bloody confrontations. Police are expected to intervene in aggressive conflicts, but that intervention should be limited and carefully controlled. Operationally, police have to decide when it is appropriate to act and how to do so.

The policing of the Marikana massacre of 16 August 2012, a disturbing industrial confrontation resulting in multiple fatalities, merits detailed attention. The Marikana massacre represents the worst episode of uncontrolled police brutality and violence since the 1960 Sharpeville massacre and, symbolically, it evokes in graphic detail the historic apartheid-era police shootings of miners in South Africa. The recalling of Sharpeville in light of Marikana is particularly chilling; it evokes the same kind of political and policing symbolism of police and communities in conflict (Petrus, 2014, p. 74). After a day of anti-pass law demonstrations by blacks, 300 besieged South African Police (SAP) on 21 March 1960 fired on a crowd of about 25,000 outside the Sharpeville police station and killed 69 people (70 per cent were shot in the back as they ran from the police attack) and injured more than 180 in what became known as the 'Sharpeville massacre'. Heavily-armed, inexperienced and inadequately trained police officers had panicked and shot more than 1,000 rounds spontaneously and indiscriminately (Frankel, 2001). The following weeks witnessed further demonstrations, strikes and riots, culminating in the government declaring a state of emergency and the detaining of 18,000 activists.

Modern-day police, unable to distance themselves from the legacy of the past, continue to be viewed as a symbol of brutal oppression and evil by black South Africans (Petrus, 2014, p. 68). Dixon (2013, p. 5) goes further by arguing that insignificant social change has maintained the structural inequalities of the apartheid era which has meant that the South African Police Service (SAPS) has failed to transcend its colonial heritage 'leaving the business of police reform begun over twenty years ago unfinished'. The 2012 Marikana massacre is depicted as the worst case of police state repression against South African workers since the African National Congress (ANC) came to power in 1994 (van Graan, 2013, p. 2).

Police in South Africa

In South Africa, police were formed to control the masses and maintain colonial rule. A few months after the South African Police establishment in 1913, it dealt with strikes on the Rand which resulted in 22 strikers killed by police (Brewer, et al., 1988). The SAP historically backed the colonial state, mine owners and capital; this allegiance remained firm throughout the century. As Brewer, et al. (1988, p. 158) states, the SAP's primary task was to control and contain black South Africans which included 'the autonomy to use considerable brutality to police the townships when protest becomes effective in threatening White political supremacy'. This legacy shapes the South African Police Service's own knowledge and work orientation (Dixon, 2013, p. 8).

A police force is often perceived as a mirror of the society that it serves and controls; police legitimacy is often viewed in terms of its use, or ability to avoid, use of force. South Africa is plagued by numerous conflict groups. Today, the SAPS, comprising of approximately 200,000 police who provide law and order for almost 52 million South African citizens, appears fragile, tenuous and under challenge. The South African nation is prone to crime, collective violence and security problems. Under the ANC, police legitimacy has been limited by increasing crime rates and private-security dominance. Despite considerable efforts by the ANC government since 1994 to implement democratic legislative changes and to reform the organizational structure of the SAPS, behaviour, attitudes, values and mores within the force still seem largely the same as those of the pre-apartheid era (Petrus, 2014, pp. 75–76). The SAPS has failed to act upon previous recommendations made by various commissions of inquiry concerning the policing of public protests and violence (Govender, 2013, p. 171). In 2006, the restructuring of the public order police unit had a detrimental impact as it lost half its members and many experienced commanders (Newham, 2014).

In 2010, the Zuma government fostered the remilitarization of the SAPS in order to confront its indiscipline and ineffectiveness. However, this became manifest in aggressive and violent responses to strikes and protests that alienated the public. The SAPS opening fire on striking workers in post-apartheid South Africa has not been a new occurrence. Deputy Police Minister, Susan Shabangu, on 8 April 2008 notoriously invoked police to pursue force when confronted by threatening individuals: 'You must not worry about the regulations. I want no warning shots... You have been given guns, now use them' (quoted in Newham, 2014, p. 60). In March 2012, the National Minister for Police announced a 'people's war against criminals' as paramilitary policing mirrored the past legacy (Newham, 2014, p. 60). This strategy went beyond the militarization of the force to a new ruthless approach towards perceived criminals. During operational duties in pursuit of the 'law-and-order' agenda, the SAPS killed 1,092 people between 2008 and 2010 (Cohen, 2013). There is evidence of a malaise of police corruption and brutality: 1,448 members of police have convictions according to a January 2010 audit (D. Smith, 2013).

Platinum mining and the wildcat strike

Platinum is central to the South African economy. In 2009, mining contributed 8.8 per cent directly and 10 per cent indirectly to the economy's gross domestic product, employing about one million people (Twala, 2012). South Africa possesses 88 per cent of the world's platinum reserve and extracts three-quarters of global platinum production (M. Smith, 2013, p. 56). A cheap migrant labour system, based on black unskilled labour, has remained part of the South African political economy. The mining industry remains exploitative and dangerous: low wages, poor living conditions, danger working underground (Ramutsindela, 2013, p. A2). The Marikana mine (near Rustenburg in the North West Province) is owned by the British mining company, Lonmin, the world's third largest platinum producer. In 2012, Lonmin employed 23,915 permanent workers, mostly at Marikana (Cohen, 2013).

In the past decade, South Africa has been experiencing an increase in the number of strike days, the length of strikes and propensity for violence (see Webster, 2014, p. 29). In early 2012, a costly, militant, six-week strike raged at the Impala Platinum mine neighbouring Lonmin (M. Smith, 2013, p. 56). On 20 January 2012, striking rock drill operators at Impala presented a petition to shift the management, but the management dismissed all striking workers ten days later. In mid-February, a subcontracted worker was attacked by strikers and died en route to the hospital. On 19 February, police opened fire on striking workers who they suspected of stalking 'scabs'. In all, three died and 60 were injured during the strike. The dispute was resolved and the men were reinstated at the end of the month (Chinguno, 2014). Violence shrouded a number of players: management, state, police and workers.

On the surface, the six-week Marikana strike was about traditional concerns of wages and conditions for miners, but a range of deep-seated grievances simmered beneath the surface – unemployment, weaknesses in public service delivery, grave socio-economic inequalities, poor worker-employer relations, and government failure to implement the 26 per cent black ownership Mining Charter. Tensions were magnified by lack of unity within the workers' movement, especially antagonism and rivalry between the National Union of Miners (NUM was created in 1982 and today is the largest union in South Africa) and the more radical breakaway Association of Mineworkers and Construction Union (AMCU) (Twala, 2012, p. 62). In 1999, almost 3,000 mineworkers left the NUM to form the AMCU (Cohen, 2013). For months prior to Marikana, the AMCU had been increasing support from among NUM discontents and challenging its power-base (van der Spuy & Shearing, 2014, p. 192). The AMCU gained the support of the machine rock drillers and also the lesser skilled miners. Union divisions are uppermost to the dispute: the moderate NUM aligned with the ANC was competing for influence and membership with the militant AMCU which has recruited heavily amongst the impoverished and poverty-stricken. The AMCU leadership assailed the NUM for collaborating with the employer, the 'enemy', by failing to support the Marikana strikers (Twala, 2012, p. 63). The NUM is closely tied to the Zuma government and the South African Police Service, which is embroiled in corruption and brutality allegations. Many ordinary members have lost trust in the NUM and its alliance partner, the ANC (Ramutsindela, 2013, p. A2). As an unrecognized union involved in a 'wildcat' strike, the AMCU, acting in support of the exploited workers, was outside the established communication, bargaining and conciliation structures (Ramutsindela, 2013, p. A2; van der Spuy & Shearing, 2014, p. 192). Hence, from a police perspective, the AMCU, outside formal industrial procedures, lacked legitimacy.

Six days before the police killings, the lowly-paid, militant rock drill operators at the Lonmin mine, at the risk of losing employment, struck for a tripling of their wage to R12,500 per month (Cohen, 2013). These operators work underground in hot, dangerous and dirty conditions. They are traditional blue-collar labourers, far removed from much of the white-collar membership of the NUM. The divided and frustrated workforce at Lonmin had lost access and faith in the institutionalized negotiation processes; union rivalry fostered lack of discipline and leadership among the workers; the intransigence of management to communicate and comprise was apparent; and there was perceived collusion between the employer and the police (Webster, 2014).

The strikers were outraged on 10 August when the NUM stated that management would only address workers through the recognized NUM. The next day, the rock drill operators marched to the NUM office from where shots were fired. On 12 August, two workers were killed in a clash with security officers, one hacked by a machete and the other burnt alive in his truck. Chinguna (2014) argues that some uncontrolled strikers, who were aware that the industrial system had evolved in violence and who were now being denied access to industrial processes, followed their own moral order or rationalization that it was acceptable to be violent during a strike. Violence and destruction at the mine necessitated the SAPS deployment, but it was to be a complex, testing and dangerous operation.

The massacre

On Friday, 13 August, police were trying to prevent the miners from entering a squatter camp to join thousands of striking colleagues (Ledwaba, 2013a). Workers refused police instructions to surrender weapons and they broke the police line (Chinguna, 2014). Two police officers and two security guards and six miners were killed in a bloody confrontation with miners in an open field west of Marikana. The police correspondence book revealed that police reinforcements came from across many parts of South Africa. Police spokesman Captain Adriao claimed that the public order police were attacked by miners, who brutally hacked the two policemen to death (van der Spuy & Shearing, 2014, p. 192; Marinovich, 2012). For the next three days, strikers occupied an outcropping of rock near the mine where they indulged in chanting and dancing, some under the influence of *muti* (Polygreen, 2012). *Muti* refers to traditional medicines or magical charms that have a 'miraculous' effect. Many Marikana miners believed that it made them 'invisible' and, therefore, indestructible in battle. Some commentators have ascribed revenge for the two police deaths as a possible police motivation for the 16th August massacre (Marinovich, 2012).

On 16 August, after police gave repeated warnings to the crowd of 3,000 mine workers to disarm and disperse, the heavily reinforced police fired tear gas and water cannons. Television footage showed police firing upon a group of workers charging towards them (Polygreen, 2012). The miners had limited escape routes; the police that morning had constructed barbed wire fences as part of the crowd management plan. These fences were erected to prevent the miners from reaching the Nkaneng settlement and police ignored the pleas of strike organizers for an opening so that workers could depart safely (Shenker, 2014). The police employed stun guns to separate the groups in order to force them to run because police argued that it was 'more difficult to conceal weapons when running than just walking away' (*News24*, 12 September 2013). In the confusion, the frenzied strikers fled in different directions.

The police at Marikana on 16 August when dispersing this group of 'wildcat' striking miners on a hill shot dead 34 and injured 78 of their number. Sixteen of the deaths, near a cattle *kraal* ('big hill'), were captured by television and press cameras. Another 18 were slain during an alleged 'killing frenzy' as they approached Klein Koppie ('little hill'), which was beyond camera range and which was located by a collection of boulders about 300 metres distant from the big hill (M. Smith, 2013, p. 54). The police had opened fire with automatic weapons and handguns against the strikers brandishing spears, sticks, pangas and machetes. The SAPS employed deadly force to disperse the strikers even though less lethal strategies of crowd management were available to the police (van der Spuy & Shearing, 2014, p. 192). A water cannon was used, but its effect was minimal as shooting commenced seven seconds after its application. Amidst panic and confusion, the massacre spanned a mere three minutes.

The police were acting in lawful discharge of their duty by dispersing the striking miners. What is highly questionable is the disproportionate level of force they employed to achieve their ends. Seven hundred police personnel from various specialized units (public order policing, the national intervention, the special task force, the tactical response team, crime intelligence, detective services and the K-9) were deployed to disarm, disperse and arrest approximately 3,000 protesters who had gathered at the *koppie* since 13 August. The plan had been to splinter the protesters into smaller groups. Under an apartheid era law of 'common purpose liability', police subsequently arrested 270 miners and charged them with perpetrating the murders of their fellow workers (see Turner, 2013, p. 296 for details). Due to societal outrage, the charges were subsequently dropped (Satgar, 2012, p. 34).

Critics have accused the ANC and President Jacob Zuma of employing the police to suppress the striking miners rather than encouraging negotiations with the employers. The President condemned the violence but refrained from criticizing the police (Polygreen, 2012). Were the police motivated by self-defence or were the killings the culmination of some premeditation? (See Twala, 2012, p. 65). It is arguable whether or not the police on 16 August had a predetermined plan of attack. They were heavily armed, carrying live ammunition, and in military deployment. Most of the 400 police on the scene carried R5 or LM5 assault rifles, weapons that cannot fire rubber bullets.

The official police response was that they were acting in self-defence. The police, state authorities and the company promoted the narrative that the violent strikers provoked the incident by charging and shooting at the police (Marinovich, 2013). General Rhia Phiyega, a close friend of President Zuma, was appointed the national police commissioner in 2012 despite a lack of police or police management experience. In a video four days after the massacre, Phiyega apparently remarked to police: 'Whatever happened represents the best of responsible policing. Thank you for what you did' (Ledwaba, 2013b). Relatives of the dead rejected her 'insecure' condolences (Ledwaba, 2013a). A besieged and defensive Phiyega told reporters that 'the police members had to employ force to protect themselves from the charging group' (Saba, 2013).

North West police commissioner, Zukiswa Mbombo, ominously informed the media on the morning of the massacre: 'Today is D-Day...we are ending this matter' (Nhlabath, 2013b). Police spokesman Adriao made similar comments on the morning of the 16 August: 'We have tried over a number of days to negotiate with the leaders...It is an illegal gathering...we'll obviously have to go to a tactical phase' (quoted in Marinovich, 2012). Mbombo upgraded the level of force to Phase Three because the miners refused to lay down their weapons; the upgrade was based on this refusal rather than it being a response based on any overt threat (Nhlabath, 2013b). The South African government website immediately exonerated the police action and condemned the miners:

> Following extensive and unsuccessful negotiations by SAPS members to disarm and disperse a heavily armed group of illegal gatherers at a hilltop close to Lonmin Mine...the South African Police Service was viciously attacked by the group, using a variety of weapons, including firearms. The Police, in order to protect their own lives and in self-defence, were forced to engage the group with force.
>
> (cited in Marinovich, 2012)

The opposing viewpoint claims that the striking miners were avoiding rubber bullets and tear gas by running at the heavily armed police task force. According to Marinovich (2012), only a small number of miners were killed by police in self defence, but during the second assault 'heavily armed police hunted down and killed the miners in cold blood'. Strikers have stated that later that day, 400 metres away at the small *koppie*, police armoured vehicles deliberately drove over prostrate miners. A policeman in the dog squad, Hendrich Myburgh, at Klein Koppie, asked a National Intervention Unit constable what was going on: 'he replied by saying they deserve to die' (Marinovich, 2013). Playwright van Graan (2013) describes the massacre in words reflecting the sentiments of the victims' families: 34 miners were gunned down in the dust by an inept, overarmed and leaderless police force.

Although police may have claimed that they were motivated by self defence, others have suggested that the killing of the miners was more premeditated (see Twala, 2012, p. 65). A fortnight after the massacre, journalist Greg Marinovich (2012), for one, rejected the self defence claim, when commenting on what happened outside the view of the cameras:

> Some of the miners killed in the 16 August massacre at Marikana appear to have been shot at close range or crushed by police vehicles. They were not caught in the fusillade of gunfire from police defending themselves, as the official account would have it.

Most of the 34 miners were shot in the back while fleeing from the police, evidence that denies the self defence contention (Satgar, 2012, p. 34).

Lieutenant General Duncan Scott, who formulated the operational plan to disperse and disarm the striking miners on 16 August, (a plan that did not entail live ammunition), claimed that the shootings were not the result of his plan:

> It is not necessarily the result of the plan that I put forward. It is individual actions that it takes to pull the trigger. That is the question that needs to be put to each individual that pulled the trigger, whether they acted in self-defence as had been briefed to them.
>
> (quoted in *Mail & Guardian*, 24 October 2013)

Scott is arguing that the original authority of the constable overrides the 'pack' mentality of police operating on mass. The doctrine of 'original authority', which has been elicited in several legal cases and commissions, establishes the common law independence of the constable (Miller, Blackler & Alexandra, 1997, pp. 52–54). The powers of the police constable are exercised in his/her own discretion by virtue of his office, irrespective of rank. As the police historian Tobias (1977, p. 247) summarized: 'The "original jurisdiction" of the constable means, it was and is still said, that no one could give him orders about the way in which he performed his personal role'. However, police commanders determine the perceived legality of industrial protests and the appropriate course of action to pursue. If police intervene during industrial disputation, the members obey the commands of their superiors and act en masse as one ordered, disciplined, regimented and synchronized entity (Baker, 2005, p. 18).

At the subsequent Farlam Commission of Inquiry, Scott asserted that lack of time and intelligence caused a greater number of deaths. He further admitted that there were too many uncoordinated police units, especially at the 'little hill'. He argued that the operation should have slowed; officers 'should have backed away to a safe distance and negotiated or reinitiated negotiations' (SABC, 2013a). The modus operandi at Marikana appears to have been uncontrolled and reckless; there was no risk assessment and feasible public order alternatives were ignored. Lethal force should be the last resort, and only implemented when appropriate and reasonable.

The perception is rife that Marikana resulted from ill-trained, ill-disciplined and ruthless police and a dysfunctional and disorganized police organization unsuited to handling large-scale public disorder. Allegations describe the police planning, leadership and operational implementation as haphazard, negligent, flawed and rash. The SAPS was embellished by the 'war on crime' rhetoric of the political elite who were disturbed by social disorder (van der Spuy & Shearing, 2014, p. 195). Paul Graham, Institute for Democracy in Africa, stated that, after 1994, public order training had emphasized the use of less lethal methods of crowd control but with Marikana 'this seems to have gone out the window. There is a real problem with training and procedures' in crowd management (quoted in Twala, 2012, p. 65). At Marikana, there were police without proper education and training in public order policing tactics and techniques. Commander Vermaak has detailed inadequate training of the public order police unit, their incomplete knowledge of legislation and standing orders, inexperienced operational commanders, limited and inadequate equipment, and insufficient information and intelligence (Falanga, 2014a; *Mail & Guardian*, 2014 editorial). Inadequate equipment placed SAPS with limited decision-making capacity and alternatives. Advanced technology and computer software should be part of intelligence-led policing (Ichikowitz, 2012). The SAPS had insufficient radio communication equipment during the Marikana operation as a result of incompatible systems (Nhlabath, 2013a).

Farlam Commission of Inquiry

The Farlam Commission, under retired judge Ian Farlam and several additional members and evidence leaders, was promptly established by President Zuma on 23 August 2012. It commenced hearings on 1 October 2012 into the strike-related violence and deaths at the Lonmin's platinum mine. The terms of reference included the 'facts and circumstances which gave rise to the use of all and any force and whether this was reasonable and justifiable in the particular circumstances' (The Marikana Commission of Inquiry, 2012). The Commission's mandate is to determine whether police instigated the massacre or whether it was the miners' fault by their chaotic and destructive strike behaviour. Although the inquiry's broad mandate is to report on the conduct and activities of all role players (SAPS, Lonmin, AMCU, NUM and the Department of Mineral Resources) from Saturday, 9 August, to Thursday, 18 August 2012, the police actions on 16 August have remained the focus of deliberations. Scant attention has been directed to the death of the two police and the two security guards the previous week (Petrus, 2014, p. 73). Questions have been raised about the objectivity, purpose and tactics of the Commission. The Commission's final recommendations may indicate whether the exercise has been either a whitewash or a purveyor of truth. The widow of a slain Mirakana miner simply requests: 'I want to know why they were shot'.

Although the Farlam Commission of Inquiry has not tabled its recommendations (as of September 2014), some deductions and insights into the police thinking and actions can be extrapolated from the evidence presented by the SAPS and its opponents. The SAPS was prepared for 16 August, but that planning was confused and inadequate. No precise plan has been developed to prevent a recurrence. General police confusion at Marikana indicates serious leadership flaws, a dysfunctional chain of command and serious flaws in the police culture. As the Commission has progressed, the police evidence has been unravelling and become contradictory.

After the massacre, senior police held a nine-day meeting at Potchefstroom. Counsel for the mining families has alleged that police colluded to design a consistent narrative of their submission to the Commission to extricate them from culpability. The official police line at the Commission has been that they were under attack on 16 August and that they had acted in self defence against the miners who reportedly had used *muti* to make themselves invincible for the pitched battle (Evans, 2013; Sosibo, 2013).

The initial police plan was to protect police and media from the striking miners by employing barbed wire and then to disarm and disperse them. This planning was ineffective and fluctuated erratically; police raised the level of force and the crisis rapidly escalated. The police deployed special task units armed with machine guns; they constructed barbed wire around the strikers on the *koppie* which provided only one avenue of escape; they failed to give adequate warning; and they opened fire on the miners returning to their homesteads (Paton, 2013). Eddie Hendrickx, a former adviser on police training, listed deficiencies in the SAPS operation amidst the frenzy and confusion: inadequacy of the police briefing of the 16 August, failure to communicate with strikers before deploying barbed wire, no written operational plan, inadequate intelligence, and the firing of tear gas and grenades without a clear operational objective (Falanga, 2014b). The senior officers were at the Joint Operations Centre; none were on the ground at Marikana.

Deputy provincial commissioner William Mpembe, in charge of operations, questioned the intensified operation plan and feared bloodshed with the miners under the influence of *muti*. On the day preceding the massacre, Mpembe chillingly predicted 'there will be bloodshed' if and when the police tried to disarm the striking miners. He asserted that police officers had been 'willing but unable to harness their negotiating skills to prevent further bloodshed' (quoted in Evans, 2013). However, there is little positive evidence of police pursuing dialogue with the incensed strikers. Another police witness claimed that he only received Mbombo's instructions less than an hour before the shootings (Nhlabath, 2013b). Dali Mpofu, advocate for the miners, theorized that police who had focused on the union rivalry might have 'misdiagnosed' the Lonmin conflict due to inaccurate details of the industrial conflict and thus policing planning was inadequate (*City Press*, 6 June 2013). In January 2014, Mpofu submitted to the Farlam Commission that 60 police personnel, including the national Police Commissioner, Brigadier Calitz, the Police

Tactical Response Team, together with the Police Minister, should be charged with murder for the death of the 34 miners at Marikana on 16 August 2012 (Xaba, 2014).

Witnesses for the deceased miners testified that police provoked the Marikana miners. George Bizos, the Legal Services Centre, alleged that the heavy police presence with their use of water cannon, tear gas and stun grenades, without warning, had triggered and escalated the problem. National Police Commissioner, General Rhia Phiyega, vehemently denied this and espoused the police tenet that 'visible policing should be a deterrent' (*City Press*, 2 April 2013). Criminologists have long debated whether police presence is a deterrent or a cause of incitement of crowd behaviour. P. A. J. Waddington (1994) argues for the former, while David Waddington (2007) maintains the latter position. Police can escalate a situation and trigger unexpected responses and consequences. Phiyega has maintained that the police had a proper plan which was disrupted, resulting in the deaths. A lawyer for the dead miners' families claimed that Phiyega, who had only been in office for 63 days, had to be seen to be acting against the strikers. TV footage shown at the Commission revealed that police opened fire on the miners, some of whom were carrying traditional weapons. Phiyega refused to accept blame: 'I cannot say those 34 people were killed by the police...and to say who was shot by whom' (*The Star*, 18 April 2013). None of the police at Marikana have been suspended or charged. This contrasts with the Police Commissioner's quick suspension of eight policemen who allegedly killed a Mozambican taxi driver in February 2012, who was dragged behind a police van after apparently resisting arrest (*City Press*, 14 April 2013). In later evidence before the Commission, Phiyega confirmed her belief that the Marikana operation was 'indeed delivered in a humane manner', despite one or two errors possibly in such a 'large operation' (*City Press*, 4 June 2013).

Police at Marikana faced a daunting and dangerous public order challenge, but there is some damning evidence that they were prepared to use considerable force to disperse the miners. On the day prior to the massacre, police requested that the health department supply four mortuary vans, each capable of carrying eight bodies, 'to be sent to the scene' as well as ordered 4,000 rounds of ammunition for assault rifles (*Daily Mail*, 25 November 2013). If not premeditated use of force, at least there was the anticipation and expectation of violence. Standing Order 262 proscribes the use of live ammunition by police and clearly states that reasonable and minimum force can only be employed upon a commander's instruction. Lieutenant General Duncan Scott, who formulated the operational plan, revealed limited knowledge of Standing Order 262 and had worked from an 'older model' (Tolsi & Evans, 2013). Operational commander Adriaan Calitz gave evidence to the Commission that he urged his officers to pursue fleeing protesters and only shoot if engaged. He claimed that he was referring to rubber rounds and 'not sharp ammunition' and only 'if the armed strikers approached them with dangerous weapons' (SABC, 2013b; Maromo, 2013). Calitz admitted that he ordered police over the police radios to 'engage, engage, engage', but he asserted that was police jargon for going forward in action – not firing live bullets (Nare, 2014a). He testified to the Commission that he did not know that live ammunition was being used during the operation; if true, this is a rather incomprehensible admission from the officer-in-charge of the operation. In evidence, Calitz claimed that he praised his officers for following his instructions on the day, not because they had killed Lonmin miners, as was alleged by some media outlets. He acknowledged that he was unaware for an hour that his officers had shot dead strikers on the 'little hill'; this indicates a basic and gross communication failure in the chain of command (SABC, 2013b).

A Northwest Air wing commander with 16 years' experience in the public order policing unit, Lieutenant Colonel Salmon Vermaak, exposed the cover up and broke police ranks by challenging the police's self-defence line and unmasked internal problems by informing the Commission that he was asked to misrepresent information about the Marikana massacre and take the blame for 18 deaths at the 'small *koppie*' (Evans, 2014). According to Vermaak, police knew that the strikers would refuse to hand over their weapons and that police advances would create violent confrontation. Vermaak claimed that the national Police Commissioner Rhia Phiyega, the North West Police Commissioner Zukiswa Mbombo, her deputy William Mpembe and Brigadier Adriaan Calitz told him to lie in his testimony. The Commission chairman, Judge Farlam, has forthrightly commented that several police officers, some senior, have given testimony that was subsequently disputed or contradicted by others: 'The police can't call a variety of witnesses to give different stories and ask us to pick which one is correct' (Nare, 2014b). This is but one instance of differing accounts and the police solidarity collapsing in the face of the inquiry. Some police witnesses before the Commission were claiming ignorance or blaming others; this is not an uncommon method of diverting responsibility in threatening situations.

Filmmaker Rehad Desai, a member of the Marikana Support Committee, 12 months after the massacre, produced footage of the massacre for the Commission that indicates that the miners were peacefully moving off the *koppie*. The footage shows armoured vehicles herding the miners in the path of the Tactical Response Team. Also, police are seen with pistols drawn prior to the alleged attack. Desai, indicating a premeditated attack, argued that this footage refuted the SAPS's official version of self defence that police spontaneously employed firearms when allegedly attacked by the miners (Tolsi & Evans, 2013).

Police tampered with evidence at the crime scene, in particular at the 'little hill', including deleting video evidence from a computer hard drive and failing to provide certain documents (Goko, 2013). In September 2013, a hard drive belonging to Lieutenant General Scott, revealed significant document concealment and manipulation by police, which gave rise to alleged attempted police cover-ups (Sosibo, 2013). Some police have admitted to the Farlam Commission that they planted weapons near the dead miners. However, the SAPS refused to 'identify any possible criminality and misconduct on part of its members despite available evidence' (Malala, 2013). Internal disciplinary systems for investigating police misconduct in South Africa have eroded; there is the need to establish civilian oversight mechanisms.

Only one mineworker witness has supported the police case at the Commission. Mr X, the mineworker turned police witness, told the hearing that the miners, armed with traditional weapons and under the influence of *muti*, wanted police to shoot them (Sosibo, 2014). Mr X claimed that two policemen were killed and one was injured during a confrontation with strikers on the 13 August. One of the police officers was hit with a gun on his forehead and the other was chopped on the back of his head with a panga (Shelembe, 2014). Mr X testified that the miners on 16 August were going 'to kill the police who defended themselves: the mine [Lonmin company] are innocent and the police are also innocent' (Falanga, 2014e).

The politics of policing Marikana

Policing is a highly political and selective activity: the state historically harnesses its authority and might to repress challenge to its hegemony. Police violence was used to maintain government and company authority at Marikana. Some commentary of the 2012 massacre was starkly couched in class terms as 'the first post-apartheid South African State massacre of the organized working class, in defence of the local and international mining bosses and their profits' (quoted in M. Smith, 2013, p. 53). Dali Mpofu, counsel for the deceased and families of the injured, poignantly depicted a 'toxic collusion' between the police, the state and the company (Falanga, 2014d; Dixon, 2013, pp. 5–6). Cyril Ramaphosa, a senior ANC figure and former NUM Secretary General with 9.1 per cent ownership stake in Lonmin, is identified as the key link between Lonmin, the police and the government (Dixon, 2013, p. 7). Newham (2014, pp. 51–53) cites a number of examples of 'high level political engagement' from the power elite who pressured the Minister of Police who in turn made demands on the police command to act decisively and aggressively at Marikana.

At the Farlam Commission of Inquiry, emails have revealed that Ramaphosa corresponded with the minister responsible for mining and the ANC Secretary General in which he advocated strong action against the 'criminals'; next day, the massacre took place (van Graan, 2013). Both Police Minister Nathi Mthethwa and national Police Commissioner Phiyega informed North West Police Commissioner Mbombo of pressure upon them by Lonmin shareholder Ramaphosa to curtail the strike forcefully to prevent 'political opportunism' by the government's opponents (Sosibo, 2013; Newham, 2014, p. 51). British-owned company Lonmin, who briefed the police twice daily, provided them with a headquarters and resources, monitors to watch the strikers and transported police units on corporate buses. Leaked transcripts have revealed politically sensitive phone calls between Lonmin executives and police commanders (Shenker, 2014). On 14 August, the company and police determined that the strike should be broken in a decisive manner. The number of police on the Marikana site more than tripled. More than 500 contracted private security officials worked closely with the police by providing CCTV surveillance, helicopters, jail cells and ambulances for the police operation (McClenaghan, 2013; Newham, 2014, p. 51). Lonmin security chief, Dirk Botes, detailed to the Commission how he provided the police with maps and information about access routes and the geographical layout to assist police operational planning. On 16 August, Lonmin security monitored the larger group, but was unable to do the same for the smaller, more militant and well-organized breakaway group of strikers (Falanga, 2014d).

Political pressure appears to have been brought to bear upon police leadership 'to close down the miners' (*Daily Mail*, 25 November 2013). Evidence has indicated that police commanders were under political pressure, both direct and indirect, to undertake the dispersion of the miners even though a number of lives might be endangered. 'Police knowledge' of the political climate, an imprecise tool of accumulated knowledge and experience, can be rationalized into a significant determinant of police decision-making and strategy. della Porta and Reiter (1998, p. 22) define it as the 'police's perception of their role and of the external reality'. The SAPS knew how the 'wind was blowing'; they were conscious of political and industrial pressure to act forcefully without necessarily being given any specific direction. The SAPS radar recognized the political dynamics that the company and the government wanted a conclusive end to the 'wildcat' strike.

According to Satgar (2012, p. 57), the Marikana massacre confirms the determination of the ruling elites to utilize even state violence, manifested by the police, to maintain and manage a deeply globalized economy. Dixon (2013, p. 7) warns of seeing the SAPS as a mere puppet of the government and the company and blames entrenched social inequalities for undermining police reform. Public order expert, Gareth Newham (2014, p. 50), instructed the Farlam Commission on 16 April 2014 of concerns that 'the police were amenable to acting in response to political and private pressure' against the strikers.

The lack of funding for lawyers representing miners wounded and arrested and families of the dead has impeded the progress and arguably the fairness of the Farlam Commission. Testimony has to be interpreted in three languages for victims' families (Xhosa, Sesotho and Tswana). A survivor of the massacre, a year into the inquiry, challenged the Commission's integrity and fairness as 'our lawyers have not been paid, but those representing the police and army are paid for by the government' (Burkhardt, et al., 2013). As one South African commentator has contended: 'Manifest unfairness arises in the eyes of the public when one side of the dispute, namely the police, is lavished with financial support and personnel, while the other is denied even the most basic support to be adequately represented' (Patel, 2013). The inquiry has been impeded by accusations of both improper and fallacious police evidence, incompetent operations and cooperation and alleged violence against some witnesses (*Daily Mail*, 25 November 2013). After two years, there is still no report or findings from the Commission that was originally meant to report after four months. The tardiness of the Farlam Commission has extenuated the tragedy and failed to provide the corrective to the crowd control methods of the SAPS.

The Commission was due to finish its inquiries by 31 July 2014 but it remains in session and intends to report in late 2014. Phase One has investigated why the massacre occurred and who is responsible; Phase Two is meant to investigate the socioeconomic and political causes that led to the horrific events. Farlam's broad and legitimate objective is to compel the state and its agencies, especially the SAPS, to publicly account for motivations and actions for what happened at Marikana. A recent amendment to the Commission's terms of reference removes the clause to investigate the government's responsibilities in the events, thereby protecting it from culpability. After two years, Lonmin executives and directors have not given evidence and many police have not been cross-examined (Falanga, 2014c).

Legacy of Marikana massacre

The strike was settled a month after the massacre when Lonmin agreed to pay increases of 11 to 22 per cent for most workers; however, vicious infighting, including sporadic killings, continued between the two unions fighting for worker allegiance (Saba, 2013). Mary Smith (2013) summarized the left's view of the strike outcome: 'The Marikana miners took on the bosses, armed police, the government and corrupt union officials and beat them'. Lonmin lost $170 million worth of output when the mine was shut from 10 August to 20 September 2012 during the strike (Burkhardt, et al., 2013). The Lonmin outcome precipitated further 'wildcat' strikes at other platinum mines where workers are demanding wage increases outside formal institutionalized bargaining procedures (Cohen, 2013; Ramutsindela, 2013, p. A2). Marikana has quickly become a symbol of resistance and a rallying stage for exploited mineworkers labouring in atrocious conditions for meagre wages.

The Farlam Commission may possibly determine whether or not the Manika massacre was the result of police self defence or a premeditated event. What we do know already is that the massacre was a brutal and horrific act of uncontrolled violence by the SAPS, one that recalls the 1960 Sharpeville massacre under the notorious apartheid regime. The tactical response at Marikana was erroneous, flawed and inadequate; confusion and panic reigned in the ranks; communication between the hierarchy and the ground police was limited; and police closed ranks for damage control to lessen scrutiny of their actions (Evans, 2013). Marikana is the narrative of an inept, poorly trained and militaristic police force unsuited to handle a large-scale, turbulent industrial dispute in modern day South Africa beset by regular public protests. The accountability and fairness of all stakeholders, but especially the police, is tested by the Farlam Commission, which itself is under question. No longer can events such as the Marikana massacre be hidden from local, national and international gaze. Social media, video and mobile camera evidence expose much that happens in the public arena, a far cry from a century ago. Public reaction is crystallized to demand inquiries to right injustices.

The SAPS were diverted from their practised public order policing protocols and practices: minimum use of force, dialogue and negotiations, and retreat if deaths appeared to be inevitable. There was no internal police investigation immediately after the massacre. When 34 are killed, police have a legal responsibility to investigate the situation (Newham, 2004, pp. 52–53). A decade of inappropriate appointments and promotions created problems within the organization that surfaced in a crisis situation. Four days after the massacre, the national Police Commissioner's statement that Marikana represented 'the best of responsible policing' did not inspire confidence in the organization's capacity to appraise and rectify its public order stratagem (Newham, 2004, p. 58).

The SAPS needs to establish standards of recruitment, selection, training, promotion, command and control of police stations. The recent remilitarization of SAPS needs to be reserved; its reputation is tarnished with accompanying credibility problems. The South African solution, according to van der Spuy and Shearing (2014, p. 201), is a holistic approach that develops policing webs of public, private and civil that establish effective policing modes that support a range of policing capacities. Policing needs to be receptive to community needs while balancing its mandate to enforce the law and maintain order. Cultural change needs to be at the forefront of public order policing reform. Post Marikana, police continue to be seen as the enemy of the black population and its personnel are in need of significant attitudinal change. The South African conception of policing should change from that of a hostile force to one that protects and serves citizens with justice and fairness.

The South African 'war on crime' rhetoric created a dangerous environment, just as the anti-communist and anti-union sentiments in the post Great War decade created a hysteria that affected the policing of protracted strikes in Australia (the subject of the following three chapters). The three fatalities in early federated Australia occurred when there was a void of accountability, both individually and collectively. Could a Marikana happen in contemporary Australia or elsewhere? Industrial disputes and confrontations are not necessarily dinosaurs of the past; protest events today span diverse, diffuse, fragmented and even transnational elements. Although remote in time and place from Marikana, the three Australian fatalities at police hands conjure some public order and crowd management lessons of remarkable symmetry. Certainly, complete denial that such incidents could happen again is dangerous unless the relevant lessons for policing disruptive crowds are heeded.

3
Death by Panic: 'Bloody Sunday' on the Fremantle Wharf

Abstract: *At Fremantle Wharf in 1919, the lumpers (wharf labourers) conducted large-scale picketing against non-union labour and the unloading of the Dimboola. On 'Bloody Sunday', police, acting upon the Premier's foolish plan and armed with batons and bayonets, confronted the lumpers at strategic points on the wharf. A lumper, Tommy Edwards, was fatally wounded during one melee with police. The strike-breakers withdrew from the wharves when police failed to effectively safeguard them. Internal police files illustrate the confusion and panic amongst the police on 'Bloody Sunday', but also the 'coolness' of key police leaders who decisively communicated with union leaders in limiting further bloodshed. The coronial inquiry into Edwards' death, despite evidence to the contrary, identified the wharfies as the troublemakers and absolved the police of blame.*

Keywords: Batons; 'Bloody Sunday'; Fremantle; Inspector Sellenger; Tommy Edwards

Baker, David. *Police, Picket-Lines and Fatalities: Lessons from the Past.* Basingstoke: Palgrave Macmillan, 2014. DOI: 10.1057/9781137358066.0006.

Traditional police response

In Australia, some of the massacres of Aboriginals have been well documented and the military and police assault on gold miners at Eureka has been well chronicled. Police violence during industrial disputes, when acting in support of employers or government, has been less well-researched and recorded. Historically, police usually responded aggressively and forcefully when requested to act by employers to provide access to and egress from workplaces. During numerous industrial disputes in Australia, police escorted strike-breakers to the workplace, the most common scenario of violence between police and unionists. Rarely were the strike-breakers themselves involved in the violence. The shearing-sheds, the wharves and the mines were the workplaces most prone to violent recourse; workers in these fields were the most disposed to resort to brute force to settle disputes (Sheridan, 1994, p. 263). Traditionally, these semi-skilled workplaces were the reserve of masculine, working-class cultures, akin in some ways to traditional masculine police culture.

The mass gathering of police and strikers has always been volatile, with potential for physical confrontation and rapid escalation of trouble. Although there was no formulated policy of repression against strikers, whenever major conflict between workers and police occurred on the industrial front, police actions were usually swift, decisive, uncompromising, ruthless and sometimes brutal. In such dual-edged confrontations, police brandished weapons and guns; shots were sometimes fired; numerous arrests occurred; police brutality was alleged; special 'outside' constables were often employed; and there was little, if any, accountability of police actions (Baker, 2001b).

Sworn allegiance to the Crown and the law and an abhorrence of public disorder have been cultivated in Australian policing values. Historically, police have been subject to both organizational dominance and the policing mandate of maintaining law and order; class and employee identification has been a limited concept for them. This is in spite of the fact that in the late 19th and early 20th centuries, police recruits came from predominantly working class backgrounds; they were predominantly male, of large physique, skilled or semi-skilled with a basic education and poorly paid (Haldane, 1995, pp. 112–113; McConville, 1983, pp. 78–87).

The 1890s and the 1920s in Australia are arguably the decades of greatest conflict between police and unions (Haldane, 1995, pp. 116–117).

Prior to the introduction of compulsory conciliation and arbitration in 1904, there was a penchant for disputes to involve direct police and striker confrontation. The 1873 Clunes riot revealed the effectiveness of community opposition against a small belligerent contingent of police escorting Chinese strike-breakers; it also raised calls for effective and 'intelligent and independent arbitrament' (*Age*, 11 December 1873; Baker, 2001d). When a major industrial dispute became prolonged and reached a stalemate, the ensuing clashes between police and picketers in Australia were often intense and violent.

With communist hysteria and paranoia gripping much of Australia's ruling elites after the Great War, police were viewed as vital defenders of freedom and legitimate power. The wharves resounded with police-unionist clashes, often the result of police protection of non-union labour. As always, police were resolutely determined to maintain their authority against any physical challenge. Beasley (1996, pp. 47–53), who describes the bitter and divisive 1917 General Strike in which many strike leaders were arrested by police, argues that wharf violence was common. The Detheridge Royal Commission endorsed the continuing existence of the labour bureau at the ports and protected preference to strike-breakers ('Nationals' or 'loyalists' or 'volunteers' in Western Australia). A record of 6.3 million days was lost to strikes in Australia in 1919 (Baker, 2005, p. 36).

Policing the troubled Fremantle Wharf

In August 1917, the Waterside Workers Union in Fremantle refused to load the *Minderoo* with Western Australian flour on the reasoning that it could reach German troops. The Commonwealth Government of W. M. Hughes determined to use non-union labour (National volunteers or 'blacklegs') on the Fremantle wharves. These 'loyalists' founded the Fremantle National Waterside Workers Union in opposition to the lumpers, who were the waterside workers employed to load and unload cargo. The two groups worked the Fremantle wharves, but the lumpers had the overwhelming support of Fremantle residents. From September 1917 to May 1919 on the Fremantle wharf, the Nationalist workers ('blacklegs') received the shipowners' preference of employment in opposition to the unionized lumpers.

The waterfront dispute hostilities culminated on 4 May 1919 when police clashed with the lumpers and townspeople. Lumper Tommy

Edwards died as a result of police actions and the conservative authorities failed to hold any police to account for his death (Baker, 2005, pp. 28–49). Edwards became the first Australian worker to die as the result of police use of force during an industrial dispute. De Garis (1966, p. 103) describes the event 'as one of the most violent and lawless episodes in Western Australian history'.

Edwards' death was the tragic culmination of the complexities of policing the prolonged Fremantle industrial dispute. The vagaries of the police operations are stark: the police manoeuvre on 'Bloody Sunday' was poorly planned, ill-conceived, inappropriate and belligerent, yet the relationship between key police and union leaders was instrumental in de-escalating the violence, limiting further bloodshed and establishing relative calm on the wharf. The analysis of the policing of this volatile dispute illustrates certain elements of public order that still resonate today, especially the significance of police and union communication and negotiation in preventing picket violence.

Much has been written about the causes and events of the lumpers' dispute. Local and labour historians, industrial relations commentators and contemporary newspapers have paid considerable attention to the dispute and the resulting riot (Oliver, 1995, pp. 171–204; Hopper, 1975; Hutchison, 2006; Griffiths, 1989; Bunbury, 2006, pp. 60–83; Williams, 1976, pp. 71–77). However, the intricacies and vagaries of policing the conflict have received limited attention and differentiation. The regulation and impact of police officers on the processes of industrial disputation have generally received scant attention in Australian historiography. Detailed, historical analyses of street-level police responses to conflicts are rare (Baker, 2005, pp. 6–8). Police decisions and actions, although not determining the outcome of industrial disputes, are often important to the procedures and processes of such conflicts as the Fremantle dispute.

Police archives provide a rare opportunity to view internal correspondence of how the police planned (or failed to plan) and subsequently handled the Fremantle affray (for instance, Inspector Mann's detailed correspondence to the Commissioner of Police, 9 May 1919). The archives also highlight the role and decision-making of local Inspector William Sellenger; his differences with the police hierarchy and the involvement of the state government. The archives provide insight into police operations and the internal competitiveness and bickering within the WA Police.

Since late 1917, protection of the Nationalist workers had been a constant and frustrating liability on police resources during the unpredictable clashes on the Fremantle wharf. Two opposing unions working the same wharf proved unrealistic and unworkable. It constituted a millstone for police, who performed duty in an atmosphere where lumpers and Nationalists were 'watching one another like tigers' (Commissioner of Police to Colonial Secretary, 4 March 1918). The *Westralian Worker* (25 April 1919) saw the bitter and regionalized struggle in polarized terms: 'the lumpers had no continuity of employment,... "scabs" having been given preference and were employed in most of the boats'. Nationally, the Detheridge Royal Commission had endorsed the continuing existence of the labour bureau at the ports and protected preference to strike-breakers. The *Westralian Worker* (25 April 1919) envisaged a triumvirate (the 'Shipping Ring' [shipping employers], federal government and police) conspiring against the lumpers. The police were expected to protect the Nationalists along two miles of wharf, an odious and burdensome task that proved a constant source of apprehension for police. The Commissioner of Police believed that this protection was only possible if the wharves were 'enclosed' (Commissioner of Police to Colonial Secretary, 16 April 1918). Despite anticipation of a major clash with the lumpers, local police preparations merely focused on requests for reinforcements if a pitched battle was to occur. The police hierarchy remained unprepared and ill-equipped for the fracas of 'Bloody Sunday' (Webb, 1994, p. 3).

Local Inspector Sellenger, a career policeman who in February 1912 unsuccessfully applied for the position of commissioner, was to be a key figure in the events on the wharf. He identified 'some trying to ferment trouble' and asserted that police were strictly impartial during the prolonged dispute. He clearly identified faults on both sides but he regarded some of the Nationalists' complaints as exaggerated. Since November 1918, Fremantle police received reports of intimidation against Nationalists, some of whom alleged that they were being 'brutally punched and kicked by lumpers' (Sellenger to Commissioner of Police, 16 November 1918). The Inspector, whose men were performing long hours and extra shifts, faced difficulties in protecting the Nationalists:

> Police are stationed at the intervals from the Railway Station to the Wharf to protect the men going to, and coming from work, and Constables are stationed on the Boats while work is going on, unfortunately it is not possible

for the Police to be at every place where the men are engaged to work or to accompany the men.

(Sellenger to Commissioner of Police, 17 November 1918).

By mid-April 1919, the conflict had reached flashpoint stage. Neither the lumpers nor the Nationalists would submit the dispute to the Industrial Court. Fremantle Lumpers' President, William Renton, was belligerently imploring the lumpers to prevent the unloading of the *Dimboola* and to force the Nationalists 'off the wharf, by sheer weight of numbers' (Sellenger to Commissioner of Police, 15 April 1919). Sellenger's correspondence to Commissioner Connell (who was appointed Commissioner in 1913 and who would preside over a police force that suppressed political extremists and strikers during the Great Depression) highlights the precariousness of police protecting strike-breakers during picketing activity. On 12 April, a revolver was found among the men; on 14 April, there was 'good deal of jostling' (Sellenger to Commissioner of Police, 15 April 1919).

Local police were conscious of their vulnerability to safeguard work on the wharves against the lumpers' numerical superiority, large-scale picketing and extensive town support. Chief Inspector McKenna admitted on the morning of 14 April that the lumpers, 700–800 in number, prevented the Nationalists from working the wharves and that the police were 'not in sufficient numbers to protect Nationalists' (McKenna to Commissioner of Police, 15 April 1919). After numerous requests for extra police, Connell cancelled all leave, called in all members on leave and enlisted mounted and foot police for Fremantle. About 170 men were available for 'immediate duty', but this figure was inadequate to deal with the estimated 700–800 lumpers. Commissioner Connell sent urgent telegrams about police lack of numbers to Inspectors Houlahan (14 April), Mitchell (14 April) and Walsh (15 April). Connell informed the Colonial Secretary (correspondence, 16 April 1919) that 'it is not possible with the number of men at my disposal to protect nearly two miles of wharf'. Despite Sellenger's requests for firearms and ammunition, the Commissioner was reluctant to acquiesce 'unless it was absolutely necessary' (McKenna to Commissioner of Police, 9 May 1919). Alex McCallum, Australian Labour Federation (ALF) secretary, prevailed on the lumpers to give him one more chance to get the government to see 'reason' in this matter of 'extreme and dangerous urgency'. Such was the direct and personal rapport between the union secretary and the local inspector that McCallum during the crisis 'had a long secret conference one night with Inspector Sellenger of the Fremantle Police' (D. F. McCallum, 1973, chapter 4).

'Battle of the Barricades', 4 May 1919

Control of the waterfront space was strongly and bitterly contested. Union leaders Renton and McCallum stated that relations between the local police and the lumpers had been positive and that, prior to May 4, 'they were on good terms with one another' (*West Australian*, 31 May 1919). However, the government, after a deputation of merchants to Premier Hal Colebatch, decided to assume control of the Fremantle wharves (*West Australian*, 3 May 1919; *Sunday Times*, 11 May 1919). Instructions were conveyed to the Commissioner of Police and the Harbour Trust to control the wharf so that the shipping companies could engage labour (Nationalists) and work their vessels. On the Sunday, the Harbour Trust, in support of the lumpers, refused to construct the barricades, and volunteer carpenters had to be obtained for the task (*West Australian*, 3 May 1919). Premier Colebatch's mislaid plan was to be one of surprise and secrecy to be implemented by the state's coercive agency, the police. However, the 'intelligence branch of the Disputes Committee' warned the lumpers of the advancing motorcar and two launch parties heading to Fremantle on the Sunday morning (*Fremantle Times*, 9 May 1919).

Police, as employees of the state and sworn law enforcers, have historically been perceived as siding with government and employer against workers (Baker, 2005, pp. 28–49). Chief Inspector McKenna recognized that 'the police were to protect them (volunteers) from any attacks' while the volunteers erected the barriers on the Fremantle wharf to exclude the lumpers. Paradoxically, he also understood that the local crowd expected police to turn a blind eye by 'standing by and allowing them to come through and do as they thought fit with the volunteers' (*Daily News*, 29 May 1919).

A chaotic and bloody climax was imminent: a hostile and enraged crowd were encountering confused and uncertain police as 'spot-fires' were erupting on the confined wharf space. Inspector Harry Mann provided police headquarters with a detailed and comprehensive ten-page report of the 'Bloody Sunday' rioting on 4 May (Mann to Commissioner of Police, 9 May 1919; Oliver, 1995, pp. 176–178). Mann's account revealed the speed with which events unfolded, the intensity of the battles and the weapons used (blue metal, nuts and bolts, iron bars, pieces of limestone).

Chief Inspector McKenna claimed the decision to hand ammunition to the police 'was simply a piece of bluff' (*West Australian*, 30 May 1919; *Daily News*, 29 May 1919). The crowd, however, was unaware whether or not this was mere bluff. According to Renton, 'the bloodshed started after the police tried to drive the crowd, and had moved them 20 yards back' (*Daily News*, 5 June 1919). There was limited confrontation between police and lumpers until Edward Brown was bayoneted by a policeman. After several shots were fired from a revolver at the Edward Street entrance, Commissioner Connell instructed Sergeant Simpson to get .303 cartridges from the station and 'the order was actually given that the police were to fire if any further firing came from the crowd' (Simpson to Constable Baker to Sellenger, forwarded to Commissioner of Police, 8 May 1919).

The crowd was forced back near 'C' shed where they confronted police marshalled in military formation and armed with rifles, bayonets and batons. Renton was knocked to the ground and Tommy Edwards, while trying to protect Renton, was clubbed with a police baton. There is some conjecture about how Edwards received his fatal blow: whether it was by baton or rifle butt (see De Garis, 1966, p. 35; Williams, 1976, p. 72; Oliver, 2003, p. 73). After the reading of the Riot Act, police were issued ball cartridges as the squad of constables faced 'the vast assemblage of frantic men and women' (*Fremantle Times*, 9 May 1919). When the police command was given to 'load' and 'fix bayonets', ALF secretary McCallum yelled: 'No! Stop you fellows ...' He ran over to the police ranks: 'Put those bloody rifles down.' The morning's events reached a critical stage near 'C' shed as the growing crowd opposing the police 'could not be held back much longer' (Mann to Commissioner of Police, 9 May 1919).

Panic had gripped both police (armed and agitated) and the crowd. The confusion in police ranks may be surmised from Constable Wilson asking Inspector Sellenger for instructions, but Sellenger replied that he had 'no' instructions. Wilson remained 'non-plussed' what to do (Wilson to McKenna, forwarded to Connell, 12 May 1919). The use of police force had rapidly escalated from batons to bayonets and even to the distribution of ammunition. The *Westralian Worker*, 9 May 1919, probably written by John Curtin, poignantly asked why some police had bayonets and who ordered them to be armed: 'the police had all the equipment of a military raiding party – rifles, bayonets, ball cartridges' in order to 'subjugate the lumpers by sheer brutality' and 'their brutal exercise of force against helpless women and children'. Faced with 4,000 people on the wharf including women and children, the besieged police 'did their best to carry out the impossible task allotted to them' (*Fremantle Times*, 9 May 1919).

The local inspector took the lead in hastening dialogue and intervention amongst the key protagonists. Sellenger took a 'bold course, and went over to the enraged crowd'. Due to the crowd's restraint, 'he was unmolested' and his suggestion that McCallum and Ben Jones (MLA) consult the Premier 'was received with approval' (*Fremantle Times*, 9 May 1919). Just as McCallum and Sellenger had met previously to discuss methods of avoiding hostilities, police and union representatives, despite the morning battles, cooperated to stem the violence. Inspector Mann recorded the vital discussions and negotiations of key players in the drama: McCallum, Jones, Connell, Sellenger and Mann himself. Mann referred to union leader McCallum as 'Mac', a friendly affirmation; the Commissioner appealed earnestly for assistance in preventing further violence. Alex McCallum, who identified the volunteers as the enemy, not the police, guaranteed that the parties would not be attacked (Inspector Mann to Commissioner of Police, 9 May 1919).

Inspector Sellenger's account highlights the importance of the on-the-spot police leadership in de-escalating the violent fervour and preventing further bloodshed. After two constables informed him that they had been 'instructed to arm themselves with ball cartridge',

> (Sellenger) crossed the road amidst a shower of stones and other missiles from all directions and endeavoured to induce the crowd to go away quietly before there was bloodshed. A number of them gathered round me and some of them begged me to speak to the crowd and they might go away quietly. I did so and informed them if they came no further there would be no bloodshed.
>
> (Sellenger to Commissioner of Police, 12 May 1919)

Sellenger 'at great personal risk, went among the mob and appealed for their leaders' (*Fremantle Times*, 9 May 1919). The *Westralian Worker* (9 May 1919) praised the Inspector's 'coolness and resource' and how 'his appearance (was) greeted with cheers'. The *Fremantle Times* (9 May 1919) praised the conciliatory intervention of both police and union leaders:

> Indeed it is a tribute to the tact used by Messrs, Alex McCallum and Baglin, on the one side, and Inspector Sellenger on the other, that such a frenzied mob – as there were three or four thousand people on the wharf by this time – were at all pacified.

After Sellenger's intercession, earnest talks commenced between Premier Colebtach, Commissioner Connell and the lumpers' leaders. Police advice and frantic discussions prevailed upon the Premier to 'withdraw the volunteers from the wharf'. Arthur Watts (secretary AWU) and Ben Jones 'appealed to the crowd to retreat'. After the Premier's guarantee, McCallum claimed that 'he had little trouble in keeping his own people in order' but the returned soldiers on the bridge, ardent lumper supporters, 'were not so easily handled' although they were pacified (*Daily News*, 5 June 1919). Most returned soldiers supported the lumper cause and were prominent in the Fremantle meetings and melees with police on the following two days (Hopper, 1975, pp. 4 & 31; Oliver, 1990, p. 22).

Some lumpers, including ex-soldiers, threw the barriers into the river and the picket bureau was wrecked. Commissioner Connell showed prudence in the face of adversity by instructing 'that it would cause further trouble if the police interfered' (Sellenger to Commissioner of Police, 12 May 1919). 'Bloody Sunday' witnessed 33 casualties, including 26 injured policemen. Once the volunteers left the wharf, 'no further action was taken by police' (McKenna to Commissioner of Police, 13 May 1919). Police sensibly accepted the lumpers' 'victory' and possession of the wharf and offered no resistance when the barricades were thrown into the harbour. There was no attempt to reassert police power, a rare occurrence in Australian policing history.

Continuing tensions

On Monday, 5 May, some violent incidents and rumours pervaded Fremantle where few police personnel were to be seen. An incorrect rumour that the bayoneted Edward Brown was a returned soldier incensed some quarters. Inspector Sellenger's reaction to a rumoured attack on the police station was quick and decisive: 'Police would not be taken at a disadvantage if I could help it and immediately I issued arms and ammunition so that if the mob attempted to storm our position we could defend ourselves'. The correspondence between the local Inspector and Commissioner Connell revealed stark operational differences:

COMMISSIONER: 'If only one returned soldier was shot, there would be no telling where the bloodshed would end.'

SELLENGER: 'I pointed out that the men had been sorely tried that day, some men brutally assaulted, myself and others being fired at and the men were determined not to be made a football of any longer.'

(Sellenger to Commissioner of Police, 16 May 1919)

Connell's instruction to Sellenger was blunt and unusual: if attacked, police were to avoid 'useless bloodshed...to quietly move away and return when the excitement was over' (Sellenger to Commissioner of Police, 16 May 1919). This instruction contrasts starkly with traditional police resolution to 'win' all public order battles in order to retain their authority for future encounters (Baker, 2005, pp. 4–8, 22, 34 & 39).

Town resentment of police was directed at the use of bayonets and at 'outsiders', rural constables who had augmented the local police (*West Australian*, 6 May 1919; Oliver, 2003, pp. 74–76). In relation to the battles of Monday evening, Sellenger, who was disturbed that police needed to protect themselves, described two constables 'being brutally treated by a mob of men' and later three 'police were brutally assaulted and injured. Police had to draw revolvers to keep the crowd at bay and a shot was fired by Constable Maguire' (Sellenger to Commissioner of Police, 8 May 1919). A procession of men 'advised' café, restaurant and hotel keepers to refuse to supply the visiting police with food. Policemen were 'hooted', but they had 'the tact enough not to return the jeers'. Perth headquarters wisely ordered the country police to return home.

The ALF Disputes Committee policed its own members to ensure the impending settlement was not threatened. On Monday, Inspector Mann and Alex McCallum engaged in telephone conversations to curtail 'matters looking very serious, you and I must take this in hand'. A meeting at King's Theatre was destined to 'keep them (men) there for the night' to safeguard the settlement. By Thursday, the dispute was settled; the Nationalists succumbed and retreated from the wharf; the lumpers resumed work on 9 May (*Sunday Times*, 11 May 1919). Seven thousand people, including fellow wharf workers and most of the Western Australia parliamentarian Labor Party, attended Tommy Edwards's funeral on the Friday. No police were seen on the streets, as none were needed to control the parade. All transport stopped for three minutes as a sign of respect (*Fremantle Times*, 16 May 1919). Remarkably, Fremantle quickly returned to normal as a working port, although some tensions lingered.

Government and police decisively lost 'Bloody Sunday'; such losses were a rarity in the history of 20th century policing of industrial disputes. During colonial times, at both Clunes (1873) and Adamson (1888), police had suffered rare defeats in industrial confrontations when they were significantly outnumbered by incensed townspeople (Baker, 2005, pp. 31–34). Police authority had been resisted, but only within the confines of the specific Fremantle port dispute. There was no perceived threat or challenge to the lawful authority of the police or government. The 'old' lumpers controlled work on the Fremantle wharf again, with the 'police force in complete sympathy' (*Fremantle Times*, 13 June 1919). All industrial disputes are ultimately settled; the timing and the outcome are the uncertainties (Baker, 2007).

Some local police lauded the 'coolness and courage' and 'coolness and discretion' of Inspector Sellenger, who in turn praised 'the gallantry of the men under the most trying conditions... the highest credit of utmost bravery of sticking to their posts' (Sergeant Simpson and Constable Baker, 7 May 1919, to Sellenger, forwarded to Commissioner of Police, 8 May 1919). However, tensions were evident between Commissioner Connell and Sellenger, who had previously been rivals for the Commissionership. Sellenger wrote that his Fremantle actions 'have been adversely commented on by some Members of the Force, and by the public, and, such comments if unchecked will be detrimental to my honour, and to my capacity as a Police Officer'. Inspector Sellenger demanded a full, open and searching inquiry into the whole debacle. If his request was not accommodated, he was determined to use his influence 'to secure a searching inquiry when Parliament meets'. However, Connell's reply was a blunt rebuttal that as no charge had been laid against Sellenger, 'a request for an inquiry is premature' (Sellenger to Commissioner of Police, 10 May 1919, and Connell's reply, 12 May 1919). Six months after 'Bloody Sunday', Sellenger was transferred against his wishes to Bunbury.

Coronial inquest of Tommy Edwards

The Coronial Inquiry, previously adjourned and conducted by E. P. Dowley with three jurors, investigated 'the death of Thomas Charles Edwards, the lumper who died as the result of injuries received in the recent riot on Victoria Quay' (*West Australian*, 30 May 1919). The inquest raised perennial dilemmas of definitions of police use of force and how much force might be justified to prevent a riot. The question of what constituted public space was also at issue. Could police legitimately exclude a group of people from the wharf, their workplace? In cross-examination, F. A. Baglin (Fremantle District Council secretary, ALF) challenged Chief Inspector McKenna as to 'why the people were being removed from the wharf'. McKenna's reply was that the Colebatch Government 'had decided to take control of the wharf, and that the police had been instructed to remove all persons who had no business there from the wharf' (*Daily News*, 29 May 1919). In contravention of the Westminster separation of powers doctrine, the Colebatch Government had instructed police to act, and they did so, although there is evidence of some hesitancy amongst the ranks. Inspector Mann reported to police hierarchy that six officers had been reluctant to order lumpers to leave the wharf. Bill Young, a Maori policeman who was respected by locals, refused to take part and hid under the wharf (Inspector Mann to Connell, 9 May 1919; Hopper, 1975, p. 54). The Colebatch Government wanted the Nationalists working the wharf; it had rushed police there in late April; and the Premier even accompanied the Police Commissioner on the abortive mission by river to the Fremantle wharf. Despite evidence of police misgivings about the likelihood of forcing the lumpers from the wharf, police officers acted as a regimented entity in attempting to enforce Premier Colebatch's solution of the dispute.

Reports of the coronial inquest, which was severely flawed by several key witnesses not providing statements, suggest that the inquiry was sympathetic to police interpretations of events. Local resident, Alfred Gregg, described it as a police 'rough-up'. Despite lumper Thomas Beveridge's evidence that the 'policeman deliberately bayoneted Brown' and despite Edward Brown himself testifying that 'the constable who had bayoneted him had lost his head', police inquiries determined that no conclusive evidence was presented of the culprit who inflicted Brown's injury. In evidence, ALF secretary McCallum stated that while he was standing on a cart with Renton, he 'saw Brown bayoneted by a policeman' (*Daily News*, 5 June 1919; *West Australian*, 6 June 1919).

William Renton, still wearing the baton mark on his head, gave evidence to the coronial inquest that just after he had been batoned, he saw Tommy Edwards 'knocked down by a man in uniform. A policeman nearby had a baton in his hand. He could not say what the deceased was struck with' (*Daily News*, 30 May 1919). However, he was in 'no doubt' that a policeman struck Edwards. Sarah Edwards, a mother of three and entirely financially dependant on Tommy Edwards, claimed that her husband's dying words were: 'A coward policeman hit me on the back of the head with the butt end of a rifle'. She alleged that earlier on that morning that a 'police constable with a bayonet accosted her and told her to get away' (*Daily News*, 29 May 1919; *West Australian*, 30 May 1919). Eighteen witnesses testified to the events of Sunday morning.

The coroner advised the jury that 'no witness had said who struck the blow' against Tommy Edwards; some witnesses asserted that 'it was a policeman' but this general term did not identify any individual. Dr Hilda Kershaw concluded that Edwards died as a result of 'a fracture to the base of the skull and haemorrhage'; the deceased 'lingered a day or two, and died'. However, she believed that the 'fracture was more likely caused by a fall than by a direct blow' (*West Australian*, 30 May 1919).

The coroner concluded that near 'C' shed 'some violence was shown to the police, and apparently police retaliated with their rifles, batons, or whatever they had available'. He stressed that the 'police did not resort to any violence until it was shown to them that stones, bars of iron, etc., were thrown at them by the crowd they were trying to drive off the wharf' (*Daily News*, 6 June 19119). In simplistic terms, the coroner described the 4 May riot as a 'regular conflict between the police who were carrying out their instructions, and a crowd who seemed determined to prevent them carrying them out' (*West Australian*, 6 June 1919). The tantalising question is ultimately who gave those instructions. Although witnesses had clearly described the police as instigators of the violent melee, the coroner identified the crowd as the troublemakers and absolved the police of blame: 'In carrying out their instructions to get the people off the wharf, the police were justified in using violence to oppose that which was offered to them' (*Daily News*, 5 June 1919). The coroner and jury of three, after ten minutes of deliberation, stated its verdict into Edwards's 'death':

> That the deceased, Thomas Charles Edwards, came to his death on May 7 at Fremantle Public Hospital from a fracture of the skull caused by a wound on the head received on the wharf at Fremantle on May 4. We are unable to say who had caused the wound. Death was accidental.
>
> (*Daily News*, 6 June 1919).

Conclusion

Whenever violence has occurred in Australian industrial history between police and unionists, police protection of strike-breaking labour has often been at the core of the confrontation (Baker, 2001b). Fremantle 1919 was no exception. Aggressive police actions on 4 May 1919 arose from the long-anticipated clash at Fremantle, the Premier's plan of action, confusion as to police orders, and police panic when faced with a large surging crowd. Despite an industrial dispute of more than 18 months, police planning for the anticipated confrontation appeared limited and ineffectual. As Inspector Sellenger's correspondence illustrates, police for some time had been stretched to the limit and were considerably outnumbered. 'Bloody Sunday' highlights the unpredictability, dangerous and inflammatory nature of close physical contact between police and picketers. The 'Bloody Sunday' riot and the police loss at Fremantle illustrate that accurate intelligence, careful planning and appropriate liaison are required if police are to keep the peace when confronted by superior crowd numbers.

Sound leadership of both local police and union organizers was vital on 4 May 1919 to limit bloodshed, but it is also vital in contemporary industrial conflicts to prevent violence in passionate and explosive situations such as the 1998 national waterfront dispute (Baker, 2005, pp. 82–137, 163–190). Premier Colebatch's 'harebrained plan', using police as partisan agents of government, should not have coerced police into precipitate and violent deeds (*Sunday Times*, 11 May 1919). Police were deployed to secure the wharf for Nationalist workers but their abortive clash with the lumpers was not ideologically driven. The conundrum of police being both officers of the Crown and unionists themselves (still pertinent today) was not lost on the crowd near 'C' shed that entreated 'the constables to remember that they belonged to the working class and "to come over to our side"'; an invitation they ignored (*Sunday Times*, 11 May 1919). According to Sergeant Johnston, 'they (lumpers) appealed to us to let them get to the Scabs, they said that they were working men and we ought to assist them' (Johnston to Inspector O'Halloran, 15 May 1919).

To avoid violence at industrial disputes, both police and union leadership must control their own people, including any 'hot-heads'. Union organizers need to manage picketers if industrial peace is to be preserved, especially when 'scab' labour is involved. The quick and decisive interaction that occurred on 4 May 1919 diffused an explosive 'flashpoint' situation and curtailed further violence. The worst of policing – the bayoneting of Edward Brown and the batoning of Tommy

Edwards – inflamed passions, but the best of policing – the 'coolness' of key police leaders – prevented further violence when accompanied by decisive union leadership. The significance of police-union communication and intervention cannot be underestimated during industrial strife or for that matter the facilitating and controlling of modern-day protests.

4
Death by Deliberate Aim: Shootings at Port Melbourne

Abstract: *The fatal shooting of stevedore Allan Whittaker at Port Melbourne in November 1928 underlined the dangers of close physical confrontation between incensed workers and armed police when police protected strike-breakers on the wharf. It is argued that police leadership moulds the approach for the controlling of volatile industrial disputes: Sub-Inspector Mossop gave the order to shoot at the fleeing wharfies and Police Chief Commissioner Blamey condoned all police actions at Port Melbourne. The 1928 dispute revealed a police hierarchy distant from working-class people and a Melburnian establishment of government, shipowners and daily newspapers supportive of police actions against perceived union excesses. These powerful conservative forces emphatically and successfully rejected all calls for an inquiry into the police shootings and Whittaker's death.*

Keywords: Blamey; Port Melbourne; shootings; strike-breakers; Victoria Police; Whittaker

Baker, David. *Police, Picket-Lines and Fatalities: Lessons from the Past*. Basingstoke: Palgrave Macmillan, 2014. DOI: 10.1057/9781137358066.0007.

Although the perception presented by the state's ruling elites in the 1920s was that major strike activity undermined the fabric of democracy and challenged the political and economic system, there has been no strike in Australia's history which has directly sought the overthrow of the government of the day by workers taking up arms. Deery (1995, p. 92) argues that challenges to the state through industrial struggles are 'successful only in rare and exceptional circumstances'. The state's determination to maintain power is best substantiated by Prime Minister Chifley's use of the military during the 1949 coal strike. Although miners could possibly 'defeat' an individual employer, they were incapable of defeating the state. Even the 1912 Brisbane general strike, confined to one state, had no chance of affecting a social revolution (Murphy, 1975, p. 62). Strikes have traditionally been concerned with wages and conditions of work; today, strikes occur in relation to job security, occupational health and safety issues, managerial policies as well as the basic economic concerns of unions.

Criminologists White and Perrone (2005) assert that police deployment to control industrial confrontations in the interests of employers has established police as partisan agents. Although not consistent throughout history, police actions at specific times and during specific conflicts have attempted to suppress picket activities, left-wing agitation and unemployment dissent (Baker, 2001b). The relationship between government and police has normally been close in such circumstances. As Finnane (1994) and Blackmur (1993) agree, conservative non-Labor governments, as well as Labor governments, have utilized police forces to quash industrial upheaval, especially when their own employees, such as railway workers, have been involved. Most industrial disputations do not involve police intervention but when a major dispute becomes prolonged and reaches a stalemate, the ensuing clashes between police and picketers in Australia have often been intense and violent. The traditionalist police response to industrial disorder has been legalistic; law and order, manifest in police control, must be maintained at all costs. According to the police control mantra, perpetrators of offences must be arrested; their obstruction to order and passage suppressed.

Police have often targeted ringleaders whom the media have labelled as potential troublemakers and subversives. Such appellation has given police at times a licence to coercively use selective dispersion and arrest to restore control. Simultaneously, this has intensified and aggravated the strikers' perception that they live in an unfair and uncaring society.

The wharves in the decade after the Great War resounded with police-unionist clashes, normally the result of police protection of non-union labour as was evident at Fremantle in 1919.

Waterfront tensions

With communist hysteria and paranoia rampant amongst Australia's ruling elites during the 1920s and the 1930s, governments of both conservative and labour persuasions, to varying degrees, were open and encouraging of police suppression of radical Marxist-Leninist influenced trade unions and their organizers. During a period of industrial unrest involving the Australian Seamen's Union in 1925, the Commonwealth Peace Officers, under the direct control of H. E. Jones, was formed with the principal design of deporting communist union officials, 'Red' Tom Walsh and Jacob Johansen. Crawford (1987, pp. 8–10) argues that political surveillance of left-wing organizations and dissidents was the Peace Officers reason for existence. Both Commonwealth and state police saw their role as curbing and eliminating union excesses, particularly on the wharves and in the mines.

In 1928, Chief Justice George Beeby of the Commonwealth Court of Conciliation and Arbitration imposed an award favourable to the industrial policy of the Federal Government which the Waterside Workers' Federation rejected. By 11 September, 90 ships around the major Australian ports lay idle. The Federal Government of Prime Minister Bruce threatened to invoke the Bruce-Latham Crimes Act amendment of 1926, an anathema to maritime unions. Victorian Labor Premier E. J. Hogan promised that his government 'would provide every Protection' to 'volunteer' workers (Lockwood, 1990, p. 238). Allegations of dirty tricks abounded in relation to keeping the strike alive – allegations by unionists that *agents provocateurs* were hired to discredit the waterside workers and impede settlement of the strike (Lockwood, 1990, p. 253). Some conservative forces called for a paramilitary force to deal with waterfront strikers (Moore, 1987). The illegal, private army of the Citizens' Defence Brigade was established in Adelaide to suppress waterside workers without fear of police or federal authority intervention. The waterfront strikes of the late 1920s around many Australian ports constituted tests of industrial strength over the employment of non-union workers.

During 1928, physical violence on the docks escalated against strike-breakers when unionists realized that victory could not be attained by traditional methods. A series of bombings shook Melbourne in October 1928 (Lockwood, 1990, pp. 270–274). Bombs, described by *The Age* (5 November 1928) as the 'introduction of exotic forms of violence', exploded at boarding houses, private residences, strike-breakers' homes and a shipping company director's house (Beasley, 1996, p. 88). The Nationalist Opposition demanded greater efforts 'to maintain law and order' and demanded 'a reward for the apprehension of the scoundrels who committed the bomb outrage' (*VPD [LA]* 2 October 1928, vol.177, p. 1908). The Hogan ministry responded with a £250 reward; the Opposition had sought £1000. At the time, the Victoria Police Force was still recovering from the consequences of the infamous 1923 Melbourne police strike. The police organization had to manage the employment legacy of many strike-breaking special constables who had remained as permanent constables after all 636 strikers had never been reinstated (Brown & Haldane, 1998).

In their fight against what they regarded as police-guarded and incompetent stevedoring 'volunteers', the waterside strikers saw themselves pitted against the Bruce Commonwealth Government, the powerful and influential shipowners, politicians, judges, the daily press and the police. Street riots, bombings, stonings, stabbings, police batonings and bashings, even killings of 'scabs' presented Melbourne in violent turmoil. The Hogan Government brought 150 extra police from the country who were stationed at the waterfront to protect the 'volunteers', but this was insufficient for Nationalist and Country Party politicians, the press and the shipowners, who advocated the deployment of 1923-style special constables (*VPD [LA]* 30 October 1928, vol.177, p. 2553; Lockwood, 1990, pp. 270–274). The 'volunteers' were afraid to leave the police-protected compound. The Port Phillip stevedores' spokesman in parliament, MLA J. L. Murphy, admitted that Italians were being 'knocked about' by the stevedores not because of their nationality but 'because they are taking the places of unionists' (*Age*, 5 November 1928).

Police have always viewed industrial disorder as a realm they must win in order to preserve law and order. Police reinforcements carried guns as well as batons; the British ships' officers had revolvers. The Melbourne wharf reached flashpoint at the beginning of November 1928. About 1,200 picketers viewed police-guarded 'volunteers' (about 4,000 had registered around Australian ports) perform their jobs. The sheer physical presence of picketers at the Graham Street railway gates prevented carters from unloading goods on the wharves. The picketing represented a significant, definite and defined political act in the bitter and polarized dispute between employer and worker.

Flashpoint: police shootings

In the early morning of 2 November 1928, special trains transporting volunteers from Flinders Street to Station Pier, Port Melbourne, were blocked by sleepers, metal bars and other objects; scuffles erupted; and strike-breakers were thrown onto the railway lines. Shipowners attempted to bring the volunteers to Prince's Pier in barges but they were fired upon at Newport. Two thousand incensed unionists, many of whom were war veterans, awaited at Prince's Pier. The union men had come to the 'pick-up' to be engaged for the day but not a single unionist was employed; only 'scabs' were selected under police protection. About 150 stevedores, contrary to their union leaders' pleas, broke a police line about 50 strong (which was used to separate the strike-breakers form the strikers) and stormed Station Pier as they rushed towards the P & O liner, *Chitral*. The strikers, 'bent on using physical violence', were approaching, rushing and chasing the volunteers at work at the cargo slings (*Age*, 3 November 1928). According to the *Labor Call* (8 November 1928, p. 9), 'the crowd simply, by weight of numbers, brushed the police aside'. Police authority and reputation, based on winning any physical confrontation and maintaining control, are tested when police encounter mass resistance; the police reaction and retaliation at Port Melbourne was swift and resolute. *The Age* (3 November 1928, p. 21) conveyed the brutality of the riot: 'Batons whirled; the leader of the rabble retired with his mouth and teeth badly battered as the result of a powerful blow from a baton wielded by a fourteen stone constable, and the fight opened'.

The police ferocity was to escalate even further under the headstrong leadership of Victoria Police's Sub-Inspector Mossop. James Morris, a respected unionist, persuaded the strikers to leave the pier to avoid clashes but Mossop called him 'a bloody bastard... struck him time and time again'. Most watersiders had alighted from the pier when the police 'viciously attacked the stragglers with batons and boots' (*Labor Call*, 8 November 1928, p. 9). Morris praised 'the actions of the whole of the Police Force I saw with the exception of the Inspector, who lost control of himself and used bad generalship ... (he) thrashed me through the gates in front of the whole of the crowd' (affidavit, *VPD [LA]*, 12 December 1928, vol.178, pp. 3271–3372). *The Age* (3 November 1928, p. 21) described 'a mob on the run' when 'the police redrew their batons and belaboured the men bringing up the rear of the fast-retreating crowd'. Some of the crowd started to throw stones; a constable was savagely kicked; and some police retaliated by firing into the crowd. Joseph Goddard, the President of the Port Phillip Stevedores' Association, declared that 'Inspector Mossop ... lost complete control of himself, and told the men to draw their guns and fire' upon the trade unionists (affidavit, *VPD [LA]*, 12 December 1928, vol.178, p. 3372). Mossop's response as police commander on-the-spot was deliberate and calculated: ' ... the sub-inspector, kneeling a yard in front of his men, emptied his revolver' (*Age*, 3 November 1928, p. 21). Approximately 20 police fired revolvers but 'at least four-fifths of them fired over the heads of the men' (*VPD [LA]*, 12 December 1928, vol.178, p. 3375). *The Age* estimated that one hundred bullets were fired by the constables. The stevedores went 'berserk' and showered the police with blue metal. The *Labor Call* (8 November 1928) made a salient point that, 'not until the crowd was in full retreat did the police deliberately take aim with the intention of killing. It was an act of sheer revenge'.

The question remains as to whether the police employment of force at Port Melbourne was merely functional, to disperse the crowd, or whether it conveyed a salutary disciplinary message, designed to teach unionists a lesson about the nature of power and class authority in 1928 Melbourne. Marxist criminologist Steve Uglow (1988) cites the 25 Gordon rioters executed and the 30 Luddites hanged, the 100 miners killed or wounded at Hexham in 1761, and the miners shot at Tonypandy in 1910 and Llanelli in 1911, as examples of the 'military solution', but these deadly assaults may also have been given to teach dissenters the power of established authority in Britain. Using force to disperse a surging crowd without intending to arrest any of them was a feature of 20th century public order policing. The baton-charge and the use of mounted officers were utilized to intimidate picketers to disperse; such force differed significantly from general police duties aimed at arrests and convictions. In the 21st century, police regularly view CCTV to make arrests after a public disorder event.

The account of the Port Melbourne shootings by the avowed anti-unionist Chief Commissioner of Police Thomas Blamey, who remained a militia officer throughout his police commission (1925–1936), was accepted by government and press as 'fully justified. There must be no half measures' (quoted in *Labor Call*, 8 November 1928). Rather than investigate Mossop's actions, Blamey commended his sub-inspector's tactics when 'hopelessly outnumbered...he had reluctantly been compelled to order the men to use their revolvers' (*Age*, 3 November 1928, p. 21). Since many constables had been struck by stones and since grave fears had been held for the volunteers at the other end of the pier, the tenacious and belligerent Blamey felt that the police had been 'quite justified'. Blamey reportedly warned that police would 'employ no half-measures in dealing with similar attacks, should the occasion arise' (*Age*, 5 November 1928, p. 10). The minority Hogan Government placed full control in the hands of the police commissioner: 'Cabinet had been entirely guided by the Commissioner in dealing with the situation from the very beginning of the shipping trouble' (*Age*, 5 November 1928, p. 10). The state government, like the police department, refused to investigate the shootings. Australian Prime Minister Bruce, advocating the maintenance of law as the 'principal duty', warned that 'mob rule and violence should not prevail' (*Age*, 3 November 1928).

The daily press supported police actions. *The Age* editorial of 5 November lampooned mob lawlessness and acclaimed police authority: 'The deed (police shooting) is one of the utmost gravity, but it is not done in defiance of the law: it was done to uphold the law'. Despite its enlightened and reformist tradition, *The Age* sought no questioning or inquiry of police actions: 'The duty of the public is to stand by the police and to trust in the police'. The paper ridiculed the mob disorder and praised the 'drastic but needful step' taken by Mossop. Police had to act decisively, otherwise 'the police force is to be regarded as a farce' (*Age* editorial, 5 November 1928). By contrast, the *Labor Call* vilified the police as 'Blamey's Cosacks' and castigated the 'press mercenaries' (8 November 1928, p. 9).

Police had carried firearms to the wharf to protect the volunteer stevedores if they were attacked. The firearms were a symbol of police power and intent: a potentially inflammatory sign to the unionists. Union leaders blamed Mossop's loss of control for ordering the shootings. His cold-blooded taunt of 'Look after your dead and we'll look after ours' added to his vilification by unionists. The *Labor Call* (8 November 1928) described Mossop as a 'Fascist leader'. Most police deliberately ignored Mossop's order by firing over the heads of the crowd. Mossop claimed that his order was to fire into the air, and then the ground.

Allan Whittaker, a former veteran who was injured at Gallipoli, and two wounded watersiders had been shot in the back while two constables were seriously injured from flying blue metal. A fellow stevedore, Jim Nagel, who intended to throw scabs 'into the river', provided this vivid account of Whittaker's shooting:

> There was a chap by the name of Whittaker, he was walking on the right-hand side of the waterfront. He got shot right through the back of his neck. The bullet came out through his mouth. I saw Whittaker fall and I turned round and said, *'You dirty bastards, are you fair dinkum?'* And I saw the constable go like that with his revolver – shoot off his arm, and I got shot right through my arm.
>
> (Quoted in Lowenstein & Hills, 1982, p. 64)

Nearly three months later, Whittaker died on 26 January 1929 as a result of a bullet wound to the neck inflicted by police. The mainstream newspapers depicted Whittaker as part of a violent rabble and his military record was never made public. Although fatalities have been few in clashes between police and strikers in Australia, Whittaker's death indicates the potentially unpredictable, indiscriminate and explosive nature of police involvement in industrial disputation. Although institutional police historian Robert Haldane (1995, p. 208) refers to the shooting of the four unarmed stevedores, he does not mention that one was shot fatally. Police use of force in any crowd control situation invokes potential and unpredictable risk. Close physical contact between police and strikers demands self-control and discipline from both parties. Today, general operational duties police, who encounter public protests on the street, are unarmed for their own safety and that of the general public, as well as to avoid heightening tensions.

The Trades Hall's *Labor Call* (8 November 1928) perceived the shootings as the ultimate weapon of the moneyed and propertied class. The Bruce Commonwealth Government, 'the armed dictator on the waterfront', had ignored the Arbitration Court awards, reduced wages, increased unemployment, intimidated union leaders, extended industrial strife 'and now the shooting of outraged waterside workers in cold blood by the police'. The working class tragedy in Australia consists of being legislated against 'in every conceivable way'; 'plundered and starved' by the bosses of industry; and finally, 'because of resistance, shot and batoned by Money Power in control of the police'. For the radical *Labor Call*, 'Money Power' expected all without question to comply: parliament, the judiciary, the pulpit, the press, the military and the police. Police were classed as pawns of capitalist authority.

The Port Phillip Stevedores' Association requested a full-scale inquiry into Whittaker's death and the other shootings, while the Australian Council of Trade Unions unsuccessfully demanded an independent inquiry on the basis that Mossop struck a union official who had managed to calm the situation but then saw police shoot unionists. On 8 November, the Opposition in parliament submitted a 'no confidence' motion against the minority Labor Government on the grounds that it had failed to take 'decisive' action to crush the strike. The Country Party demanded more police (Lowenstein & Hills, 1982, p. 64). After the demise of the Hogan ministry, the McPherson Nationalist Government assumed power on 22 November 1928 and bluntly rejected all calls for an inquiry (Wright, 1992, pp. 154–155). Chief Secretary, Dr Stanley Argyle, who had successfully propositioned Blamey to accept the police commissionership in 1925, refused Labor Opposition calls for an inquiry into the police shootings:

> I am satisfied that the police did not act improperly on the occasion, but were compelled to resort to the use of firearms to maintain law and order. I am, therefore, of opinion that no good purpose would be served by holding an inquiry into the action of the police.
>
> (VPD [LA], 11 December 1928, vol.178, p. 3299)

Dr Argyle gave a passionate defence of armed police duty and order maintenance against an 'example of savagery':

> It was the proclaimed intention of the mob to attack the bureau labourers. Had the police failed to fire on the mob, which was already attacking them with missiles, and thus failed to protect the bureau labourers, they would have failed in their duty.
>
> (VPD [LA] 12 December 1928, vol.178, p. 3377).

Police are depicted as the bulwark against anarchy and mob rule. The Chief Secretary claimed that police fired to protect the free labourers on Prince's Pier, but ex-Premier Hogan queried whether any free labourers were actually there (VPD [LA] 12 December 1928, vol.178, p. 3379). The Labor Opposition argued that the refusal to hold an inquiry was 'unprecedented' and that Dr Argyle was acting as 'both judge and jury in the case' (VPD [LA] 12 December 1928, vol.178, p. 3370). Labor MLA Murphy for Port Melbourne produced three statutory declarations from eyewitnesses to the shootings which condemned the role of Sub-Inspector Mossop who 'unfortunately lost his head' in the fracas, but generally the constables remained composed (*VPD [LA]*, 12 December 1928, vol.178, p. 3271). The Labor Party call for an inquiry focused on the direct role and orders of Mossop. Part of the rationale for an inquiry was that 'men in the Police Force will be lying under the stigma that they attempted to take life when really the only man responsible for the whole thing was the sub-inspector in charge at Port Melbourne' (*VPD [LA]*, 12 December 1928, vol.178, p. 3273). During the previous 1917 industrial ferment, police had controlled 'the excited crowds without resorting to shooting', but not so in 1928. Concern was raised about Blamey's public opposition to any form of inquiry: 'If the Chief Commissioner of Police is satisfied that the right and proper attitude was taken by the officer in charge of the police at that time, why should he fear a public inquiry?' (*VPD [LA]*, 12 December 1928, vol.178, p. 3274). Despite the contrary opinions, there was no investigation to ascertain the truth of what precipitated the shootings and riot – whether it was caused by police firing their revolvers to protect the free labourers or whether it was provoked by the caning of Morris by Inspector Mossop.

The coronial inquiry shed little light on the circumstances of Whittaker's shooting. The fact that three other workers were shot on the pier was not even considered. The police version was that Whittaker was shot in the face and that the bullet escaped through his neck. Medical evidence indicated that he was shot in the neck while fleeing the police. No waterside workers were ever questioned about the riot. The coroner concluded 'justifiable homicide – by gun' and condoned the police action of firing into the surging crowd. The policeman who pulled the trigger was never named (Garritty, 2010). Individual police and the force's reputation were being protected. Former Supreme Judge Frank Vincent has examined the inquest documents and concluded there was a cover-up: 'At best, the inquest emerges as surprisingly superficial in its investigation...and, at worst, as suggesting a deliberate avoidance of the full exposure of what had taken place' (quoted in Silvester & Rule, 2010).

The police department, the Chief Commissioner, the Inspector-in-charge and the justice system were never held to account for the shooting. Victoria Police conducted a secretive internal inquiry but it was never released to the public. To this day, the official records of the shootings in the Chief Commissioner's file correspondence for 1928 cannot be located at the Victorian Public Records Office (Haldane, 1995, p. 333). The loss of internal documents, the lack of any external inquiry and the indecisive and flawed coronial inquest established an inertia, as the government and the police hierarchy continued to pursue their hard-line and belligerent approach against striking workers. Government and police remained steadfast in protecting individual and collective police actions against allegations of excessive police force during industrial disputes. This unwillingness to investigate and remedy any police excesses was safeguarded by newspaper approval of the 1928 policing at Prince's Pier.

Opposing forces of police and strikers clashed at various ports over the contentious employment of free 'volunteer' labour. Port Adelaide witnessed major industrial rioting on 28 September 1928. By the next day (unlike Victoria where Blamey claimed his men showed that they could handle the situation), 2,000 Special Constables were organized to prevent disorder and resist violence on the Port Adelaide waterfront. Like Victoria, South Australian police were under a military Commissioner, Brigadier General R. L. Leane. In January 1929, various clashes occurred between wood, stone and bottle-throwing wharfies and baton-wielding and mounted police; on one occasion (18 January) mounted police were led by Leane himself. Allegations abounded of the too frequent use of the baton 'by some younger policemen'. The Port Adelaide Trades and Labour Council claimed that 'a baton should only be used as a last resource, and the Commissioner of Police, is not under law, an infallible authority to deprive citizens of their rights' (quoted in Budd, 1990, p. 142). By contrast, former South Australian Chief Superintendent Budd (1990, pp. 142–143) labelled the Port Adelaide mobs as vicious, violent and undisciplined.

Blamey and Leane were both battle-hardened, pragmatic soldiers whose policing philosophy with working-class dissenters, especially with perceived communist-inspired connections, was to stand, resist, suppress, prevail – then talk (Budd, 1990, pp. 137–144). The appointment of experienced military commanders as police commissioners enhanced the inherent links between the two organizations. Both the police and the military institutions celebrated coercive powers, the male culture and brotherhood, the 'code' of loyalty, and operated in a void of public scrutiny and regulation (McCulloch, 2001, pp. 15–31). Finnane (1994, p. 37) asserts that, during the turbulent early decades of the 20th century, police commissioners, prone to determine what constituted acceptable social order, were inevitably involved in defining the police role in management of industrial disputation and 'some commissioners at least were only too ready to engage'. Blamey did not so much engage in political debate over industrial unrest but rather he championed his anti-union philosophy both within and outside the force and gave his officers unquestioned support in repressing picket and protest activity. According to Hetherington (1973, p. 63), Labor politicians viewed Blamey as 'an arch-disciple of reaction, an adherent of the Establishment aligned with the bosses against the workers'. Historian and serving officer, Robert Haldane (1995, p. 208), depicts Blamey's public order style as quick to side with capital against labour and being 'confrontationist, readily violent, and generally ruthless'. McCulloch (2001, p. 45) states categorically that Blamey, while Chief Commissioner of Police in the late 1920s, simultaneously headed the secret, pseudo-fascist White Army in Victoria. Cathcart (1988) discusses rumours about his dual role identity while biographer Horner (1998, p. 97) argues that there is still no conclusive evidence that Blamey was the organizational head of the White Army's predecessor. Both Blamey and Leane received full government support, which meant that the actions of their officers received no legal or official scrutiny. The major union losses and port closures of 1890, 1917 and 1928 had dire consequences for the unions; however, the legalistic police policy and aggressive, paramilitary strategy remained intact and fortified.

The polarized nature of political and economic life in the late 1920s placed police in positions of inevitable physical conflict with workers during times of industrial strife. As police belonged to disciplined organizations directed by authoritarian leaders, they were prone to violent outrages such as the event that occasioned Whittaker's death. Grant and Wallace (1991, p. 1123), from their study of violent strikes in Ontario from 1958 to 1968, stress the need to research 'the role of the counter strategies' such as police in determining the sources of violence (not just the strikers). The authors illustrate that there has been 'no rigorous, quantitative study of strike violence in advanced industrial countries in the post-World War II era'. They refer to the highly legalistic approach of Canadian employers to labour-management conflicts and their willingness to use the legally sanctioned coercion of police to escort strike-breakers across picket lines to maintain plant productivity (Grant and Wallace, 1991, p. 1125). Repressive legislation at times, such as the 1928 Bruce-Latham Transport Workers' Act in Australia which gave preference to strike-breakers, may have heightened the fury of police-picket clashes but it has been the employment of strike-breakers, dependent on public police protection, which has commonly occasioned violence between police and workers as transpired at Prince's Pier in November 1928.

Conclusion

Police eagerness to show their political masters their capacity to smash picket lines, especially by escorting strike-breakers, can escalate an already volatile situation and act as the 'flashpoint' to spark confrontation (D. Waddington, 1992 & 2007). Employers customarily relied on the apparatus of the state to assist their plants to remain open and to protect staff and strike-breakers. Police command, aware of prevailing political and industrial climates, knew implicitly when they had a strong mandate to act directly and aggressively. Police and union capacity to negotiate and compromise limit the chances of violence, but such dialogue and liaison was non-existent during the waterfront disputes around Australian ports in the late 1920s.

Historically, police, salaried guardians of the state and professional law enforcers, generally sought to establish their perceived order by fulfilling employer demands. Given a more clearly-defined independence from government and a greater diversity of responses, police law enforcement need not have always been so inflexible, so doctrinaire and so confrontational as in 1928. The conservative press supported police actions against overt signs of industrial unrest and, at times, 'criminalised' the militant union agitator. Whenever government and press condoned police coercion against strikers as occurred in 1928, there ensued little, if any, internal or external scrutiny of excessive police actions.

Despite early exceptions, police usually 'won' the major violent confrontations with picketers in Australian history, including contests on the wharves (Baker, 2002). There remains a resolute and determined approach by modern police authorities to control major industrial turmoil, either by persuasion or the perceived threat of coercion. The policing of the 1998 national waterfront dispute presents a much more discriminatory, non-confrontational and sophisticated approach by police than most historical cases of policing industrial discord (Baker, 1999a). The authority to use force remains, as it did in 1928, but that force today must be reasonable in the circumstances and open to scrutiny.

General Blamey's unconditional support for Sub-Inspector Mossop's leadership not only affected public order at Port Melbourne but also enhanced union perception that policing, despite its advocacy of neutrality, enforced a rigid law and order that supported employers' requests to the detriment of workers. The very ingredients lacking during the 1928 dispute were apparent in the communication and protocol between the Victoria Police and the Maritime Union of Australia in 1998 – policing independence from government; developed police-union protocols and liaison officers; willingness to negotiate and compromise; an omnipresent electronic media; and both police and union leadership determined to avoid violence (Baker, 1999b). These were safety valves that were missing in the explosive industrial cauldron of 1928 Port Melbourne. Nevertheless, the police function remains constant as one of control; today, compromise between police and union leadership may occur, but the workers still remain the ones to be policed.

5
Death by Misadventure during the Rothbury Riot

Abstract: *The death of coalminer Norman Brown at Rothbury was the result of a ricocheted police bullet amidst a chaotic scene between police and workers during a bitter industrial conflict. Heavily outnumbered police, prone to panic, indiscriminately fired weapons at Rothbury on 16 December 1929. A flawed coronial inquest was conducted into Brown's death; it disregarded miners' evidence about the police shootings and no concerted effort was made to unmask the culprits. After the Rothbury riot, violent and brutal clashes erupted on the Northern NSW coalfields. The enraged mining communities blamed the 'basher gangs' or 'outside' police for the repression and violence. As the state government championed the police actions, there was no public inquiry into either Brown's shooting or police violence on the Northern coalfields.*

Keywords: 'Basher gangs'; coroner; Inspector MacKay; Norman Brown; Rothbury riot; shootings

Baker, David. *Police, Picket-Lines and Fatalities: Lessons from the Past*. Basingstoke: Palgrave Macmillan, 2014. DOI: 10.1057/9781137358066.0008.

The Northern coalfields dispute

Akin to the deaths of Edwards and Whittaker, the tragic shooting of Norman Brown at the Rothbury colliery on 16 December 1929 highlights the precarious nature of the policing of industrial lockouts or strikes and the dangers posed by close physical contact between police and agitated unionists. The Battle of Rothbury was but one day in a 15-month industrial struggle by more than 10,000 miners and their families in the New South Wales Northern region. At the outset of the Depression, the policing of Rothbury and more generally the Northern coalfields 'signalled a new ferocity in the policing of labour disputes' (Williams, 2007, pp. 20–22). On 16 December 1929, Norman Brown, aged 28, miner of Greta, was shot and died later that morning in Maitland Hospital. The *Daily Telegraph Pictorial* (17 December 1929, p. 1) described the 'sensational fight' as 'the most dramatic industrial clash that has ever shocked Australia'. Prime Minister Scullin lamented that the dispute 'should have developed into violence and the injuries should have been afflicted by Australians, one upon another, in an industrial dispute' (*Sydney Moring Herald* [hereafter *SMH*], 17 December 1929, p. 11). Although Brown's death was lamented by many across Australia, there was no public inquiry and many questions remained about the veracity of the coroner's inquest.

The Nationalist Bavin state government encouraged police use of intimidation and force to achieve its industrial and political agenda. Police were compliant and willing to assist the owners and the state government's preoccupation in re-opening the Rothbury colliery, a steep seam mine subject to explosion in 1925. In solidarity, the miners' communities fought to prevent the re-opening of the Rothbury colliery and the incursion of the 'outside' police. A pitched battle mentality was evident in much of the policing of the Northern NSW coalfields in late 1929 and early 1930.

State governments to varying degrees encouraged and expected police suppression of radical trade unions and their organizers (Baker, 2005). Major and prolonged industrial disputes in the 1920s reflected the declining impact of judicial arbitration and the rise of bitter strikes and lockouts. NSW in 1929 faced the timber strike in Sydney and the coal lockout in the Northern coalfields (Evans, 2005, pp. 114–118). The timber strike pitted aggressive militant unions against employers and a dogged state government. Violence ensued; 22 men were convicted of acts of violence against strike-breakers; 16 received jail terms (Evans, 2005, p. 118). Police

Superintendent MacKay was ordered to deal with the unrest; he quickly commissioned a centralized, mobile force, based on speed and surprise, to control the timber strikers. Strikers retaliated by staging mass pickets at particular timber yards and threatened street disorder, an affront to police authority. MacKay's mobile force became the blueprint for the 'flying squad' (the basher gang) on the Northern coalfields that would physically intimidate the rank-and-file miners, including the raiding of meetings and inflicting of beatings (Evans, 2012, p. 183). The timber and mining industrial disputes provided the opportunity for the NSW Police organization to demonstrate its relevance and substance for the state government.

The protracted and prolonged lockouts on the NSW coalfields endured from 2 March 1929 to 3 June 1930. Industrial discontent among the aggrieved miners had been rife in the Hunter Valley coalfields for months. However, the Northern coalfield lockout was relatively calm and remarkably peaceful, but tense, for ten months prior to the arrival of 'outside' police and the Rothbury riot. Production had been declining throughout the 1920s (Gollan, 1963, pp. 177–187). Owners demanded 12.5 per cent reduction in worker wages, and colliery managers demanded the right to hire and fire. All Northern coalfields worked by union labour stopped production and gates were closed to lockout the workforce. Considerable hardship engulfed the communities (*Smith's Weekly*, 25 January 1930, pp. 8, 11). Jim Comerford, a 15-year-old pit boy at the time, provides a graphic and detailed eyewitness account from a miner's perspective of the 15 months' lockout in *Lockout* (2006).

The NSW Coalition, led by Premier Bavin and the Minister for Mines and Forests Reginald Weaver, the latter nicknamed 'The Rajah of Rothbury' by the unionists, were determined to defeat the miners by advocating the use of strike-breakers ('volunteer' or 'free' labour) in the mines. In September 1929, Premier Bavin stated that he would use force – the state police – to open the Rothbury mine, close to Branxton township. The state government, acutely aware of the coalfields' unrest, legislated the Unlawful Assembly Act and deployed 'outside' police. From November onwards, Weaver was resolute and determined to open just this one mine, Rothbury (Comerford, 2006, p. 323). He was widely quoted as boasting: 'Even though the Heavens will fall, we will open Rothbury' and 'We will "go" the miners', the latter remark he vehemently denied (*Kurri Kurri Times*, 19 December 1929). At an aggregate meeting, the general secretary of the miners' union, echoing the Great

War rhetoric, viewed Rothbury as 'the storm centre. It is going to be the frontline of the trenches' (quoted in Hawke, 1999, p. 1).

Opportunities were re-offered to former employees to work, but on reduced wages. Aggregate union meetings rejected 'the November Compromise' of the Bavin government (Comerford, 2006, pp. 305–319). The miners' leaders were divided over whether to accept or reject the terms of settlement offered in December: members of the Rothbury Lodge generally favoured acceptance of the terms while the New Greta Men rejected the terms. In December, the state government called for 'miners, wheelers, youths, engine drivers and casual labour' to work the mines and guaranteed police protection of these volunteers, a common duty for police when strike-breakers are escorted to a work-site (*Kurri Kurri Times*, 12 December 1929). Weaver's visit to the goldfields and the government's determination to reopen the Rothbury colliery with contracted volunteer labour, 'a foolhardy enterprise', constituted a direct challenge to those miners who had been locked-out (*Newcastle Morning Herald & Miners' Advocate* [hereafter *NMH&MA*], 17 December 1929, p. 7). A potential bloody confrontation was imminent: the existing arbitration and conciliation institutions were failing or being bypassed; the men's wage grievances were acute; the police were well aware of state government expectations; and senior police appeared very willing to adhere to those wishes by escorting and protecting strike-breakers through picket-lines.

On 13 December 1929, a special train that conveyed about 40 'free' labourers and 40 policemen arrived at Rothbury. Colonel Boardmore established a camp with 18 large tents and five marquees. As local police were deemed untrustworthy to handle the tense mining stalemate, the 'outside' police were deployed to the region to roam the streets of the mining towns to impose compliance. The police were housed in tents in bushland south of the colliery manager's house while the officers were quartered in his own house. Both police and volunteers used the colliery bath-house facilities. These 'outside' police, housed and drilled in military formation were remote from the local community, and even from local police, and were perceived as an adjunct of the mine owners. Despite the new Mass Picketing Act, the mine-owners feared that mass picketing would come into operation with as many as 5,000 men involved (*Sydney Morning Herald*, 14 December 1929, p. 18). Three hundred and fifty non-unionists or 'blacklegs', under heavy police protection, were drafted to work the Rothbury seam, the approaching storm-centre (Gollan, 1963, p. 195). Hostile confrontation was imminent between an aggrieved workforce in impoverished circumstances that was pitted against a government and mine-owners who were hell bent on reopening the Rothbury mine with 'muscle' provided by a compliant police force.

The Battle of Rothbury, 16 December 1929

The aggregate miners' meeting of Sunday, 15 December 1929, resolved to prevent 'scab' labour working the Rothbury mine. At the various meetings, lodge leaders had sought an orderly, peaceful protest. Although lacking planning and preparation, estimates of 5,000–6,000 mobilized miners from Cessnock, Kurri Kurri and other coalfields marched through the night to reach Rothbury at daybreak on Monday morning to mass picket the colliery, with the intention of maintaining a smaller picket indefinitely (*SMH*, 17 December 1929, p. 11). In festive spirits, the 'army' was headed by a pipe band, with singing and joking, bonfires and billies on the boil (*Kurri Kurri Times*, 19 December 1929). Coalfields newspaper correspondents described this dawn gathering of miners as being akin to a picnic crowd.

The hostilities began at 5.30 A.M. when miners destroyed fencing in order to invade the Rothbury colliery. Miner Wal Dawson described the impasse at the colliery fence where there 'were lines of police, so we ranged up, facing them'. When the volunteers refused to leave, 'so over the fence we went' (Dawson interview, 1978, p. 2). Superintendent Alexander Beattie, officer-in-charge of the Newcastle police district, confronted them 'with about 40 police' and warned them to leave. When the miners continued to advance and after he was struck by a stick, Beattie ordered a baton charge. He instructed his officers that 'they had batons with which to protect themselves, and revolvers to protect themselves against armed malefactors' (*Maitland Daily Mercury*, 12 February 1930). Hundreds of miners had penetrated both the colliery fence and momentarily the police defence, but 'eventually the police gained the upper hand', as foot and mounted police, used batons ferociously (*Cessnock Eagle*, 17 December 1929, p. 1). Local state MLA for Cessnock, Jack Baddeley, persuaded the men to retreat and calm pervaded for some hours.

The initial battle resulted in three miners wounded by rifle fire, and some constables hurt by flying stones and wood. Police reports alleged that three shots were fired and that police retaliated by drawing their revolvers, firing into the ground, injuring the miners as a result of ricocheted bullets from the ground (*SMH*, 17 December 1929, p. 11). It was reported that the police 'fired about eighty shots into the air and along the ground', although there are conflicting interpretations that some fired low, directly into the crowd (*Cessnock Eagle*, 17 December 1929, p. 1). The quandary of what constitutes 'absolutely necessary' use of force was debatable and subjective in 1929, just as it is in the modern era of Marikana.

Around 9.30 A.M., there was a renewed, and more violent, sortie to enter the Rothbury colliery, but on this occasion the police were prepared and resolute although still heavily outnumbered by the miners. The miners 'were infuriated' but again forced back during this 'more serious clash' (*NMH&MA*, 17 December 1929). When Inspector Jack's car, falsely believed to be carrying Weaver, appeared at about 10.30 A.M. en route to the colliery, 'there was a general rush by miners on one side and police on the other. Before the car moved into the enclosure, shots were fired by the police' (*Maitland Daily Mercury*, 12 February 1930). Miners with sticks hurled stones at police who 'fired their revolvers and dispersed the crowd'. It was during this melee that Norman Brown, on the fringe of the crowd, received a fatal bullet wound either in the back or in the stomach. Others were seriously wounded (nine received bullet wounds); and several police were hurt (*Kurri Kurri Times*, 19 December 1929). Eyewitness Jim Comerford, a youth at the time, graphically recalls the wounding of 21-year-old Wally Woods whose right side was paralysed for 18 months:

> The choked noises in his throat, his feet drumming the ground, the blood running from his throat. And I saw the bloke that did it. He had leather leggings on, police uniform, and he deliberately aimed the revolver at Wally Woods.
>
> (ABC PM radio interview, 1 May 2006).

Some miners, 11 of whom were arrested, had torn up the colliery railway line.

When informed of the fracas, the acting Commissioner of NSW Police, Walter Childs, immediately dispatched reinforcements to Rothbury: 150 volunteers and a police detachment of 79 police left Sydney by special train in the morning after news of the initial pitched battle at Rothbury; and another 110 police were deployed by train to Rothbury in the afternoon (*SMH*, 17 December 1929, p. 12).

After the announcement late in the morning that the Chief Justice of the Arbitration Court, Justice Dethridge, had convened a compulsory conference with Justice Beeby as presiding officer, 'the men dispersed, and quietness was restored' (*NMH&MA*, 18 December 1929, p. 7). The conservative *Sydney Morning Herald* (17 December 1929, p. 11) stated that this announcement prevented an 'even worse clash between picketers and armed police later in the day'. Twenty miners and nine employees, alleged to have participated in the confrontation at Rothbury would subsequently appear in the West Maitland Court on Tuesday, 21 January 1930. They all emphatically denied the police evidence and refuted the charge of 'knowingly continuing in an unlawful assembly' (*Labor Daily*, 22 January 1930, p. 3).

The blame game

Allegations were made that some miners had fired the first revolver shots (*Daily Telegraph Pictorial*, 17 December 1929, p. 1). The *Daily Telegraph Pictorial*'s special correspondent (17 December, 1929) observed that Superintendent Beattie with about 20 police 'without recourse to arms' ranged themselves in slight cover about 50 yards within the fence and forced back the assault by drawing batons to club the miners, and 'during the affray three shots were fired by the miners'. However, Labor MLA George Booth of Kurri Kurri retorted that this was not so, as not a single policeman was injured by a revolver shot, and no miner fired a shot (*Kurri Kurri Times*, 19 December 1929). Similarly, Comerford (2006) was puzzled that miners were hit, but not a policeman. Miner Alf Purcell recalled 50 years later: 'There were no guns on our side – no one expected shooting to happen' (quoted in *Common Cause*, 1978, p. 2).

Superintendent Beattie on the morning of 16 December telephoned Police Commissioner Childs with the news that, after rioters had fired the first shots, he had 'ordered the police to draw their batons and charge the crowd'. Childs immediately reported that 'shots were fired by the mob, but the firers could not be identified'. Comparable to the validation of the police behaviour at Fremantle (1919) and Port Melbourne (1928) by the two police hierarchies, Childs defended the operations of 'individual members of the force [who] have acted with commendable restraint and discretion' and he reiterated 'every confidence in Superintendent Beattie' (*SMH*, 17 December 1929, p. 11). He appealed to the reinforcements of 'the necessity for coolness, tact, and restraint in dealing with the situation' on the coalfields (*NMH&MA*, 17 December 1929). Premier Bavin on the same day wholeheartedly commended the police who 'have acted throughout with the greatest restraint and moderation, and I cannot speak too highly of their conduct' (*NMH&MA*, 17 December 1929, pp. 6–8). Weaver released a statement in support of Superintendent Beattie, that failed to mention Brown's death, but that extolled 'the remarkable patience and tact exhibited by the police under him' (*SMH*, 17 December 1929, p. 11).

The city newspapers criticized the unionists, condoned police actions, and subsequently rejected any accountability of individual or collective police batonings and shootings. The pro-capitalist *Sydney Morning Herald* (17 December 1929, p. 10) defended police actions in using batons and revolvers in the emergency and condemned the miners. The vehement anti-union *Smith's Weekly* (25 January 1930, p. 10) encouraged much stronger government and police action against the ringleaders of the revolt and incited revenge upon anyone who 'unlawfully interferes with his fellow citizen' by advocating that such a person 'be knocked on the head'. Premier Bavin's action was derided only for delaying 'too long' as he dithered 'while the country famished for the coal lying there under his hands'. *Smith's Weekly* (21 December 1929, p. 8) condemned union protest for inviting 'all the thugs, bashers, gangsters, loafers, wasters, and bludgers against whom the police have to defend the common cause'. The thin blue line is depicted as unimpeachable as it defends capital against unionism.

In stark contrast, a number of eyewitness union officials and miners contradicted the official police account that the miners used revolvers. James Connell, check inspector and representative of the Miners Federation at Rothbury, was one who challenged the police reports and vehemently denied that shots were fired by the miners. Wal Dawson and other Rothbury veterans have always bluntly denied the Government's story that there was shooting 'from both sides...there were no guns on our side; we swung our fists as best we could and some maybe had waddies – but no guns, and we were up against guns and batons'. The miners believed that the Government had 'used police to try to beat the miners into submission' (Dawson interview, 1978, p. 2). Neither journalists nor eyewitnesses at Rothbury reported any shots being fired other than those fired by the police (Evans, 2005, pp. 131–132). The newspapers of the local mining communities were much more sympathetic to the locked-out miners than their city counterparts. Local newspaper correspondents agreed with eyewitness miners' accounts that contradicted police reports that the miners used revolvers (*SMH*, 17 & 18 December 1929, p. 9 and p. 15 respectively). The *Cessnock Eagle*'s correspondent (20 December 1929, p. 1) claimed that the police falsely issued reports that miners had used firearms at Rothbury.

Polarized responses to the riot and Brown's death quickly crystallized opposition in the NSW Parliament. On the afternoon of 17 December, the Premier described thousands of miners prepared to take possession of the colliery and violently expel the volunteers. Courageous police, who performed 'duty, well and nobly', after endeavouring to persuade 'the men to go away', only drew and fired their revolvers as a last resort when their own lives were endangered (*SMH*, 18 December 1929). Weaver argued that the mass of miners who trekked through the night to reach Rothbury at 5.30 A.M. to intimidate the volunteers, conspired to overwhelm the police, annihilate the free labourers, and destroy the camp and the mine (*SMH*, 18 December 1929). He further alleged that the Opposition and miners groups 'were using the death of the young man, Norman Brown, for propaganda purposes... to deliberately inflame the men on the field'. The Secretary for Mines defended the police 'who only acted on the execution of their duty. They should not be called murderers because they were defending themselves' (*NMH&MA*, 20 December 1929).

The Opposition led by Jack Lang moved a motion in Parliament deploring the death of Norman Brown and condemned the Government for 'permitting the use of the police to further the efforts of the mine-owners in their attitude of open defiance of the law'. He saw the villains of the affair as 'the coal-owners, backed by the revolvers of the Government police, who have defied law and order' (*NMH&MA*, 18 December 1929, p. 8). The Legislative Assembly accepted part of the motion that referred to Brown's tragic death, but rejected the section censuring the Government. Lang asked telling questions that still resonate today when police use lethal force to quell a crowd or mob (certainly pertinent to the 2012 Marikana shootings):

> Who told the police to shoot?... Who ordered them to discard tact and use bullets? Who could do it but the Government, which was determined according to its mouthpiece (Mr Weaver) to 'go the miners'. Did the police fire in self-defence? Were their lives in danger?
>
> (*SMH*, 18 December 1929, p. 16)

Labor MLA George Booth, who was at Rothbury 'from start to finish', told the House that 'the miners never fired a shot at all ... and the first shot fired came from the police'. Booth demanded a 'full and open inquiry' into Brown's death: 'We do not want an official inquiry; we want a public inquiry, conducted by men who will give a clear and impartial verdict' (*Cessnock Eagle*, 24 December 1929, p. 1). It never transpired!

Superintendent MacKay himself was highly critical of some of the police incompetence and signs of panic at Rothbury, including Beattie's 'disastrous' role in failing to meet the challenge (Evans, 2005, p. 133). Better police planning for Rothbury and more flexible tactics would have helped the police operation. Mounted police, though an effective public order tactic to move stationary protesters, would have taken days to assemble at Rothbury. The police hierarchy's headstrong agenda to suppress the miners and appease the mine-owners and government made violent confrontation inevitable. Evans (2012, p. 192) contends that if police had remained calm and permitted union officials to control the miners, the tragedy may have been avoided. This is feasible, except that historically whenever police escorted strike-breakers to a workplace, antagonism between police and workers was enflamed. Evan (2005, p. 133; 2012, p. 192) highlights the poor senior police planning and leadership augmented by Weaver's ideological obstinacy in creating the Rothbury tragedy. To the locked-out miners and their communities, police protecting strike-breakers were agents of a repressive government. Panic-stricken by being grossly outnumbered, some police resorted to excessive use of force by firing revolvers on stone-throwing miners.

Norman Brown's funeral attracted the 'largest crowd ever seen in Greta', a remarkable tribute, a crowd that included Superintendent Beattie and Inspector McKay, both despised by the miners (*Cessnock Eagle*, 17 December 1929, p. 1). The attendance was estimated at between 6,000 and 7,000 grim-faced miners while the 'business houses in Cessnock and Kurri were closed during the afternoon as a tribute to the memory of the deceased' (*NMH&MA*, 18 December 1929, p. 7). The Bishop of Newcastle, Dr Long, eulogized that Brown was not engaged in any breach of the law or riotous conduct, but a casualty, an accidental casualty, in a bloody confrontation, 'from our strivings where, unfortunately, the innocent fall under the penalty and suffer punishment' (*SMH*, 18 December 1929, p. 15).

Continuing police-miner hostilities

The Rothbury riot, itself the culmination of months of industrial unrest and rumour, acted as a catalyst, a spark for further intense bitter confrontation between police and unionists in the early months of 1930. Regular violent clashes occurred between mass pickets and the escalating police deployment who generally failed to exhibit restraint on the Northern coalfields. A Canberra journalist professed that only 'the ruthless rule of baton law' prevented an armed industrial war. Locals asserted that the violence was confined to 'outside' police (see Dixson, 1983, pp. 136–141). Comerford (2006, p. 4) argues that Brown's death 'served to demonstrate again that the power of the state would be used to intimidate workers who were fighting for their rights and to crush any evidence of rebellion in defence of them'. Police were, and are, the coercive arm of the state; there may have been no individual intent behind Brown's killing, but the general tone of policing on the NSW coalfields suggested a willingness and a ruthlessness to appease government and owner. Premier Bavin instructed police 'to take all possible steps' to end dissent and food relief was only made available to men 'who obey the law and who refrain from taking part in any demonstration, breach of the peace, mass picketing or unauthorised drilling' (*Cessnock Eagle*, 14 January 1930, p. 10).

The occupying police were often depicted as either arrogant or tense. The *Labor Daily*'s (20 January 1930, p. 5) first dispatch by its Special Correspondent in the Rothbury camp highlighted the polarization and hatred between 290 police and the miners: 'But there is no love lost here. The police hate us. They hate Rothbury, and we keep them here. That's why they hate us.' The ratio of two police to one miner in the camp was overwhelming. A police officer was reported as asserting that the militaristic police defence of Rothbury 'was impregnable' against any civilian attack because its security was 'carried out on military lines, with barbed wire entanglements, two machine guns, rifles, and revolvers' (*NMH&MA*, 11 January 1930). Further violence at Rothbury was constantly anticipated: 'police, pickets, residents generally, and visitors were very nervy yesterday, fearing a repetition of tragedy such as occurred on 16 December' (*NMH&MA*, 11 January 1930, p. 7). Special police wireless equipment for transmitting and receiving, and additional personnel detachments, augmented police dominance. The Labour Council formed the 'Workers' Defence Army' for protection 'against the ambushing of miners' and there were rumours on both sides of civil war (*SMH*, 18 December 1929, p. 16).

A week after Brown's death, there was relative peace, but tensions escalated when police raided the homes of union officials in Kurri Kurri when searching for bombs and ammunition (*SMH*, 23 December 1929, p. 11). Ten thousand miners and trade unionists demonstrated at Cessnock against the Bavin Government's obstinacy in employing non-union labour. The *Cessnock Eagle* (24 December 1929) reported that 'private detectives were scattered amongst the crowd...half a dozen detectives were seen working off the ground at the close of the meeting' who were 'hooted by the crowd'. Detectives were used to guard the railway and train loads of coal produced by the strike-breakers at Rothbury (*Labor Daily*, 10 January 1930, p. 1).

The NSW Police mobile 'flying squads' were prone to terrifying the mining communities of the northern NSW coalmines by suddenly and unexpectedly appearing from buses, cars and motorcycles, with batons drawn to attack mass bands of miners (*Kurri Kurri Times*, 16 January 1930). MacKay's men harassed the miners, raided homes, disrupted union meetings and even committed assaults on locals. The police baton attacks, increasingly regular and vicious, were justified by the enforcement of the Mass Picketing Act as many miners were charged with being members of an unlawful assembly. On 12 January 1930, police, 'subjected to much hooting' and stone-throwing, charged a large crowd with batons at Kurri (*Maitland Daily Mercury*, 13 January 1930).

Three days later, a 'flying squad' of police in automobiles arrested lodge officials and batons were freely used in what was described as 'the wildest scene in the history of Kurri Kurri' (*NMH&MA*, 16 January 1930). The Kurri miners and residents 'had no complaint to offer against the Kurri Kurri police who watched the proceedings without interference', but despised the 'flying squad' who conducted 'a wild rush with drawn batons', so brutal that even some local police 'shouted out to them to desist' (*NMH&MA*, 16 January 1930, p. 6). Previously, local police had peacefully supervised union meetings, but this episode was a ruthless baton-wielding display of police dominance by one hundred constables under Beattie and MacKay's command. Mining lodge officials sent an urgent telegram to Prime Minister Scullin that demanded federal protection from MacKay's men: 'Peaceful citizens of Kurri Kurri ruthlessly attacked by police, batons freely used, request protection of Federal authorities' (*NMH&MA*, 16 January 1930; *Labor Daily*, 16 January 1930, p. 1). The Kurri community deputation requested the withdrawal of the 'outside' police reinforcements to prevent 'further bloodshed, as well as loss of life. The visiting police were inflaming the minds of the people, and in their absence there would not be any trouble' (*Maitland Daily Mercury*, 16 January 1930). Cessnock alderman, Snedden, described the police as 'Bavin's Bulldogs', as 'cruel and heartless beasts', and accused the 'flying squad' of having 'slogged into men old enough to be their fathers' (*Cessnock Eagle*, 17 January 1930). The *Labor Daily*'s special reporter opened his account of the 'basher gangs' confrontations across the Northern coalfields of Kearsley, Bellbird, Hebburn, Abermain and Weston on 15 January 1930 with this condemnation of the police brutality:

> In a wild orgy of baton charges by the flying squad of the police on the coalfields today scores of defenceless and law-abiding miners were clubbed into insensibility. Every attack was unprovoked, and was launched by the police without warning.
>
> (*Labor Daily*, 16 January 1930, p. 1)

On the same day, MacKay's ruthless 'flying squad' won encounters at both the Abermain No.1 and No. 2 mines (*SMH*, 16 January 1930, p. 11). These police victories reinforced the policing dictum that police must win all public order confrontations in order to maintain their future authority and control (Baker, 2005, pp. 28–44). Such deliberate, aggressive and fierce police actions, under the command of Superintendent Beattie and Inspector MacKay, effectively quelled much miner unrest.

Newspaper accounts are riddled with military metaphors and references to the policing of the Northern coalfields. On 10 January, 10,000 miners were on the march across the Maitland coalfields 'spied upon and irritated and threatened by an army of police', but 'not one policeman was molested'. The *Labor Daily* (11 January 1930, p. 9) argued that because 'not a drop of blood was spilled...this proves that the miners are not an irrational, unruly and undisciplined mob of wild men thirsting for blood' as the anti-working class press portrayed them (*Labor Daily*, 11 January 1930, p. 9).

The solidarity and ire of the mining communities affronted the police contingents. The South Maitland coalfields citizens protested against the government action 'in employing the police to protect the property of the coal-owners, who have flouted the awards, and thus caused the shooting down of the workers' (*NMH&MA*, 21 December 1929, p. 7). The Cessnock sewerage employees condemned police 'in shooting down our defenceless comrades at Rothbury', and they pledged to provide the miners with 'moral and financial support in order to bring this struggle to a successful conclusion' (*Cessnock Eagle*, 20 December 1929). During the Kurri march of 10 January 1930, the miners marching in step who had 'not forgotten their military training... were loudly cheered by large numbers of women. As the police approached silently, the womenfolk shouted and hooted at them' (*Labor Daily*, 11 January 1930, p. 1). The Miners' Federation declared 'black' any hotel or business 'serving or accommodating police or persons connected with the working of Rothbury' (*Labor Daily*, 10 January 1930, pp. 1, 3). The Cessnock Municipal Council not only urged the Premier to withdraw all police, 'with the exception of the local police', but also requested the 'federal government to give the people adequate protection *against* the police' (*Cessnock Eagle*, 17 January 1930).

On 21 January 1930, a deputation from the Northern coalfields, comprising business people, clergy, shire councillors and miners' representatives, met with the Chief Secretary, F. A. Chaffey, 'for the purpose of urging the withdrawal of the police drafted into the district'. Miners maintained that the 'outside' police, not the local constabulary, intimidated and threatened mining communities. The deputation insisted that local police 'were quite capable of dealing with the position, and undertook to find a guarantee of £5000 that there would be no disorder if the police were withdrawn'. The Chief Secretary rejected both requests on the basis that police 'were an honourable body of men' who had been assaulted while performing their duty at Rothbury (*NMH &MA*, 21 & 22 January 1930, p. 5).

Historian Robin Gollan (1963, p. 196) concluded that police 'seem to have conducted themselves with an arrogance and brutality that went far beyond the requirements of maintaining order'. Miriam Dixson (1983) describes the aftermath of Rothbury as 'one of impending civil war' as local communities treated police as an army of occupation; hoteliers refused to serve them. Festering discontent and poor morale amongst police aggravated the ruthless police sorties. The police, failing to receive a pay increase, tired of their role on the coalfields. A fortnight after Norman Brown's death, the secretary of the NSW Police Association, P. Fortescue, reported conditions for police were 'somewhat unsatisfactory' as a 'result of the rush' to deploy them and he acknowledged that Rothbury 'is not a nice place for long duty'. Poor sanitation, unsatisfactory tent accommodation and food, flies and mosquitoes added to the police's disquiet, plus the constant fear of miners adopting arms (*Maitland Daily Mercury*, 6 January 1930; *Labor Daily*, 20 January 1930, p. 5).

The anti-communist hysteria of the times, prevalent amongst the authorities, was manifest in the trial of German communist organizer Joseph Shelley, who was sentenced to two months' imprisonment for inciting to murder at Kurri Kurri. In the Maitland Police Court, Shelley gave full vent to his political dogma: 'Norman Brown did not die in vain. He was shot down by parasites – tools of the capitalistic system' (*Cessnock Eagle*, 14 January 1930). In testimony, Sergeant Lake claimed that during a year of mining trouble 'there was no disturbance till the communists came on the coalfields'. Joseph Shelley's defence counsel retorted to Lake's accusation that the 'trouble coincided with the arrival of the police on the fields' (*Labor Daily*, 25 January 1930, p. 5). Championing anti-communist and anti-unionist rhetoric, the NSW *Police News* magazine, two months after the Rothbury riot, lampooned the 'despicable tactics' used by the 'Reds' at the Rothbury colliery and argued that the strong police coalfield presence prevented 'civil war – the aim and hope of vicious and foolish communists' (Williams, 2007, p. 21). The police were portrayed as the thin-blue line preventing 'an orgy of anarchy and destruction' (*SMH*, 20 January 1930, p. 10).

Whitewash: coronial inquest into Brown's death

In January 1930, the Maitland District Coroner, D. W. Reed, adjourned the inquest into Norman Brown's death for a month due the 'very unsettled state' of the region. Reed's decision provides evidence of the hostility and tension within the mining community:

> If publicity be given to the incidents of the fateful 16th of December, by a recital here, and by the publication in the Press, it may have the effect of causing further ill-feeling in the community, which is not desirable in times like these.
>
> (quoted in *Maitland Daily Mercury*, 13 January 1930).

The pressure and anticipation of a large crowd of locked-out coalminers who had surrounded the courthouse probably influenced the coroner's ruling to adjourn (*Labor Daily*, 14 January 1930, p. 1).

The coronial inquest into Brown's death resumed in mid-February and continued for five days. The records of the coronial inquest have not survived, but detailed reports exist in the *Newcastle Morning Herald & Miners' Advocate*, *Cessnock Eagle*, *Labor Daily*, *Maitland Daily Mercury*, and

Sydney Morning Herald. Fifty-three witnesses gave evidence; mostly miners and police. J. Clancy appeared for the relatives of the deceased and the Miners' Federation, but found himself in heated dispute with Coroner Reed (*Maitland Daily Mercury*, 13 February 1930). On one occasion, he chided the coroner's anti-worker bias that was apparent by the fact that whenever he, Clancy, got a witness 'to contradict himself, I am fired at from two quarters – my friend and the Bench' (*Maitland Daily Mercury*, 13 February 1930). W. J. Curtis appeared on behalf of the Crown and police, and staunchly defended and exonerated police actions at Rothbury. The opposing legal representatives challenged the validity, interpretation and sensationalism of newspaper reports. Curtis attacked as an outrageous misrepresentation the *Labor Daily*'s leader 'Shot while Playing Cards at Rothbury', while Clancy bridled at Curtis's statement in the newspapers that Brown was shot by a fellow miner (*Maitland Daily Mercury*, 12 Feb 1930). Throughout the inquest, the coroner, who described the outraged miners as 'an unlawful assembly at common law', consistently used highly emotive language such as 'rioters' and alleged that the miners used 'such force and violence [against the volunteers] ... to alarm persons of reasonable firmness and courage' (*NMH&MA*, 18 February 1930, p. 8).

The core of the miners' accounts were consistent; similarly, police evidence was constant; but the testimony overall was conflicting and contradictory. Both sides closed ranks during the inquiry. The miners saw one thing; the police saw another. The miners' evidence generally alleged that Brown was shot in the back by a policeman, but no witness was able to identify the individual policeman who fired the fatal shot. A Kurri miner, John Lindsay, asserted: 'I believe he was shot in the back' (*Cessnock Eagle*, 11 February 1930). Greta miner, James Dever 'said that he saw a policeman aim directly at him [Norman Brown] ... he never saw any miners armed'. However, Dr. Douglas Stewart conveyed an expert's theory that 'the bullet entered the stomach and came out at the back' (*Cessnock Eagle*, 11 & 14 February 1930, p. 1). Ballistics expert Major Horace Robinson testified that it was a 'spent bullet' that ricocheted twice that entered Brown (*NMH&MA*, 14 February, p. 5; *Maitland Daily Mercury*, 11 February 1930). A number of miners stated that a policeman deliberately aimed at Brown; this was refuted by all police witnesses. The miners asserted that since no miner was armed, therefore no miner fired any shots; several police, however, claimed that they saw armed miners (*Maitland Daily Mercury*, 13 February 1930). Plain clothes sergeant Robert Munday testified that 132 shots were fired across the two encounters.

This indicated the police's willingness and determination to combat and overwhelm the unionists (*Maitland Daily Mercury*, 13 February 1930).

In summation, Clancy referred to the police witnesses as 'like perjury parrots', singing from the same protective hymn-book. In accord with the miners' evidence, Clancy concluded that Brown 'was shot while running away, that he was shot with a police .45, and that the police fired unnecessarily long'. Curtis for the Crown concluded that 'Brown was accidentally shot by a bullet during an unlawful assembly at Rothbury' and that shots were fired by miners as well as police. Curtis incredulously introduced a new political element in his defence of the police: he accused the Communists of being 'the murderers of Norman Brown'. Curtis scathingly attacked the 'Reds' because 'if the "Reds" were eliminated there would be peace in the industry' (*NMH&MA*, 14 & 15 February 1930).

Brown's death was classified as accidental stemming from a bullet ricocheting off the ground. Coroner Reed considered that the 'deceased was a bystander and not a partaker of the riot, being quelled at the time, and that he was accidentally shot' (*NMH&MA*, 18 February, p. 8). Contrary to much testimony, the coroner exonerated the police of any wrongdoing. Reed determined that the police 'carried out their duty with forbearance and commendable restraint' and applied necessary force to prevent the rioters reaching the colliery. His support of the police account was unwavering; miners' evidence that police aimed at the crowd, was dismissed as 'incredible', but the coroner failed to provide any evidence or rationale to reject the evidence of several miners that police fired deliberately at the retreating crowd (*Cessnock Eagle*, 18 February 1930, p. 1). The coroner failed to identify who fired the fatal shot or the cause of other serious wounds. The inquest was a whitewash; much in the style of the other coronial court judgments exonerating police actions in the fatal cases of Edwards (1919) and Whittaker (1928) during industrial confrontation.

Nationalist Premier Bavin rejoiced in the coronial outcome that exculpated the police officers of the malicious charges. He confidently asserted that 'all law-abiding Australian citizens [would] read the findings with pleasure' (*Maitland Daily Mercury*, 18 February 1930). NSW law and order triumphed, but justice did not prevail. A ricochet police bullet killed Brown whose death may have been accidental, but the police's orchestrated attack on the miners was not. In the NSW Legislative Assembly nearly a year later, MLA Booth was persistent and resolute in demanding 'a full and comprehensive inquiry into Rothbury ... [and] into the activities of the police ... [and upon] whose authority were the baton charges made on law-abiding people?' (*NMH&MA*, 12 December 1930, p. 6). Despite expectations of union supporters that the newly elected Lang Labor Government of November 1930 would instigate an inquiry into the policing of the coal lockout, it never eventuated (*Labor Daily*, 1 November 1930, p. 6).

Conclusion

Like the 1919 and 1928 maritime conflicts, virtually all industrial disputes are eventually settled, but they vary as to length and outcomes (Baker, 2005). After 15 months and increasing poverty, the locked-out Northern coalminers returned to work on basically the owners' terms, although unionism, including the Miners' Federation, survived the loss (Turner, 1976, p. 84). The coalminers resumed work on reduced contract and pay rates: 12.5 per cent reduction for contract workers and 6d per day for day labour colliery workers but the men did not lose any other benefits (*Maitland Daily Mercury*, 16 May 1930). MacKay's 'flying squad' no longer patrolled the coalfields 'but would never be forgotten'; local police mixed again with the people, but the relationship remained strained (Comerford, 2006, p. 430).

Together with the deaths of Tommy Edwards (1919 at Fremantle) and Allan Whittaker (1928 at Port Melbourne), Norman Brown's tragedy has become part of the labour movement's folklore, but these deaths also represent an epoch in Australia's industrial history when unionized workforces were confronted by headstrong and powerful establishments consisting of conservative governments, employers, police and mainstream press. Neither Royal Commission nor parliamentary inquiry nor criminal trials were conducted into the deaths of the three unarmed men. There appeared to be no concerted effort to unmask the protagonists and the motivation behind the three fatalities. There was no attempt to discover the truth. Norman Brown's death epitomized the intrinsic dangers of government and police collusion during major industrial disputation, and prompts permanent questions about excessive use of police force. Heavily outnumbered police prone to panic and following inflexible tactics, indiscriminately fired weapons at Rothbury. The police mindset, led by the tough and driven Inspector MacKay and enforced by the 'outside' police, employed excessive force against the locked-out miners on the

Northern coalfields. There was little middle ground for communication and negotiations during the protracted lockout: the authorities blamed the miners for the violent confrontations; the unions blamed the state government and the NSW Police for their repression. Brown's death was the last fatality as the result of police force during industrial disputation in Australia. The fact that there has been no fatal repetition in succeeding decades indicates some advances in avoiding the use of excessive, lethal force.

6
Lessons for Managing Pickets and Protests

Abstract: *Positive lessons can be gleaned from the failings of the traditional policing of the three Australian fatalities at police hands and from the recent Marikana massacre in South Africa. Key concerns for police include: dialogue and communication between police leaders and union organizers to prevent violence; more flexible and transparent police planning to avoid surprises; improved communication amongst police ranks; and operational policing decisions that are independent from the dictates of involved parties to the dispute and from government collusion. If police coercion is necessitated, it must be reasonable in the circumstances, the minimum level necessary, and a violence de-escalation plan in place. The tragedies central to this book underline the necessity of police accountability when dealing with industrial confrontation and public disorder.*

Keywords: Accountability; best practice; communication; lessons; violence

Baker, David. *Police, Picket-Lines and Fatalities: Lessons from the Past.* Basingstoke: Palgrave Macmillan, 2014. DOI: 10.1057/9781137358066.0009.

All industrial disputes are eventually settled; the length of the dispute and the conditions of the settlement are the variables. Many disputes require no police intervention; it has been, and remains, the exceptions that create particular challenges, difficulties and dilemmas for police. Universally, the police mandate involves the control and order of public space. Police are determined to always 'win' contests if their public order authority is perceived to be challenged.

Approximately nine decades apart, the three Australian historical fatalities and the Marikana massacre constitute extreme case studies of wanton and unnecessary deaths, partly attributable to uncontrolled and frantic policing. The deficiencies of police tactics and behaviour are apparent in these extreme cases. Therefore, they provide relevant and valuable lessons for rectifying such problems and improving the dynamics of the interaction between police and unionists, or protesters more generally. Issues of power, use of force, leadership, accountability, government interference and media pressure were pertinent to policing operations at the time of the three Australian fatalities effected by police coercion. Such issues still resonate today in South Africa and other countries prone to violent police interaction with workers.

When police found themselves heavily outnumbered against union agitators on the wharves and the coalfields, some panic materialized in police ranks as they resorted to arms, with fatal consequences on three occasions in Australia. The police actions were condoned, even supported, by the respective police hierarchies, state governments of the day and the mainstream newspapers. The police leadership of the 1920s mirrored the hardline conservative and reactionary governments and the mainstream press that were consistently anti-communist, anti-unionist and even anti-worker. On these tragic occasions, police, an essential institution, acted as protectors of the status quo and enforced government policy. Government, police hierarchy and 'outside' police labelled unionized miners and wharfies as dangerous, treacherous and even potentially incendiary revolutionaries. The state police organizations and leaders seized the opportunity to improve their standing and enhance their influence with the government of the day (Weinberger, 1991). Coronial inquiries were held into each death, but they were essentially a whitewash. Neither Royal Commission nor parliamentary inquiry nor criminal trials were conducted into the deaths.

These three Australian fatalities portray some common characteristics:

- all occurred during a prolonged and bitter era of class warfare and anti-union and anti-communist hysteria;
- strike-breakers constituted an affront to unionized workers;
- police were ill-trained and inadequately managed;
- police were never held to account for any excessive actions;
- the wharf and coal-mining communities were closely knit and supportive of fellow workers during the industrial conflicts;
- the unions involved were noted for their solidarity, masculinity and toughness as their numbers, like police, worked in dangerous occupations.

Marikana obviously occurred in a different industrial era and country. The SAPS acted from a background prone to police-worker violence due to the apartheid policing legacy, the limited reform of the organization, the political and company pressure upon police to act decisively, the inadequate police training and tactics, and the confused and chaotic police chain of command and communication.

Some factors help to clarify the causation of violence between police and union picketers. The likelihood of violent interaction is increased if the dispute is prolonged and protracted; if broader injustices and long-standing grievances are evident; if the conciliation and arbitration mechanisms are non-existent or fail to operate adequately; if police are unduly 'pressured' by employer or owners or government to take decisive and aggressive action against strikers; if police are escorting 'scabs' to the workplace or protecting them; and if police and unionists have a history of violent encounters (see D. Waddington, Jones & Critcher, 1989).

Failings of the past

Traditionally, when police actively intervened to suppress strikes in Australia, they usually did so in an aggressive, belligerent and punitive manner (Baker, 2005). If their authority was challenged, police responses were usually quick, forceful and even brutal. The traits of violent confrontation were not just apparent in 1920s Australia but could also be applied to certain policing aspects of the Marikana strike in August 2012:

- The police attitude was one of 'us v them'; the protesters were perceived as the enemy that needed to be brought under control.

When police knew little or nothing about a group of strikers, police easily and quickly perceived them as the 'opposition'.
- Armed police could be a recipe for disaster as police, especially the inexperienced and ill-trained constables, became panic-stricken when confronted by a milling and angry large-scale crowd.
- As police public order training and planning was often non-existent, a resort to force became the default strategy when police found themselves outnumbered by a hostile crowd.
- Neither communication nor liaison took place between police leaders and union organizers. Inspector Sellenger's dialogue with union representatives at Fremantle, both before and on 'Bloody Sunday', was exceptional for the times.
- Many senior police leaders were former military commanders, whose anti-unionist sentiments coalesced with the political climate. (For instance, former Generals Blamey and Leane in late 1920s Australia, and the remilitarized SAPS commanders in 2012).
- Police, especially 'outside' police, were distant, even hostile, to local communities, who rejected them as unnecessary and intimidating.
- Many unionists perceived police as too closely and willingly aligned with government and employer structures.
- The institutionalized structures failed to conciliate and settle the industrial conflicts.

Lessons in the Western world have been learnt from the aggressive and legalistic policing of the past (della Porta, et al., 2006; Baker, 2012). The increasing levels of police accountability, both collectively and individually, have affected policing of public disorder including pickets and lockouts (Sarre 2001, p. 64). Today, scrutiny of police behaviour spans mobile television cameras, private mobile phone cameras, internal investigation departments, internal reviews, ombudsman's office, judicial review, civilian oversight bodies and civil litigation.

'Best practice' recommendations

Best practice approaches are dependent on variables, only some of which are within police control and others that are not so. A key dynamic of any large-scale demonstration is the interaction between police, protesters, bystanders, citizens, media and potential protest targets. Police responses to a protest event can either inflame or diffuse a potentially violent situation. Reicher (2011, p. 20) argues that the 'facilitation rather than repression should be the default option' until evidence exists that 'relevant individuals are pursuing a course of disruption'. Modern-day, pragmatic police leaders in the Western world are aware of the risks of attempting to crash through mass picketing. Increased police professionalism and heightened mass communications make the police-union nexus more open and accessible. Today information collation, evidence gathering, video surveillance and negotiation are vital to police management of industrial strife (Baker, 2007a & 2014).

Worker violence, even if in a valid cause, erodes public sympathy and support just as police coercion can do. Unions may be generally accepted for safeguarding employees' economic and working conditions but they are vilified if industrial action turns violent. Unlike 1919 (Fremantle), 1928 (Port Melbourne) and 1929–1930 (Northern NSW coalfields) and especially since the contemporary advent of mobile television and private phone cameras, police and unionists have appreciated the value of avoiding physical confrontations, thereby preventing injury to one's members and avoiding negative publicity. Each side has learnt from past experiences: neither police nor unionists want injured members; neither wants bloodshed; neither wants to face litigation; and neither wants extensive media coverage of violent and unlawful actions. In modern-day Australia, police legitimacy depends on willing societal consent and cooperation; union success is tied to community support and public opinion (Baker, 2001c & 2007a). The same lessons need to apply in South Africa.

Scholars are divided whether police should enter negotiations with protesting crowds or picketers: Smeltzer argues against it while Spiegel advocates civilian intermediaries to parley with crowds (see D. Waddington, 2007, p. 59). On the contrary, della Porta, et al. (1998 & 2006), D. Waddington (2007) and Baker (2014) argue that concerted police emphasis on police dialogue, liaison, communication and negotiated management with protesting crowds or unions lessens the likelihood of escalating violence. Although negotiated arrangements may be initially fragile in police-crowd encounters, although some suspicion, uncertainty and disruption is inevitable, although organizational structures and ideological outlooks are diverse and although police have the power to change plans to accommodate an evolving scenario, it remains in the self-interest of both police and unionists to facilitate peaceful protest through meaningful dialogue, whenever feasible. Negotiated management fails if uncompromising picketers or protesters refuse to acknowledge protest limits and engage in direct action by assailing institutions, threatening basic infrastructure or taking over the streets. It also fails if police renege on agreements. Police commanders, whose objectives may not easily coalesce with the rhetoric of facilitating peaceful protest, fear the loss of control and order in public space (Earle & Soule, 2006).

Dialogue initiatives create opportunities for negotiated arrangements that set parameters and expectations for crowd behaviour, limit surprises and establish some rapport. In the unpredictable and multi-faceted interaction between police and picketers, dialogue can nurture a constructive relationship and lessen the extent of aggressive and confrontational policing. Dialogue with crowd organizers, by fostering communication, negotiated agreements and conflict mediation, provides some degree of legitimacy and order to large-scale protest and the opportunity for peaceful dissent. In Australia, the negotiated approach between police and protest organizers has found a positive response from the more enlightened institutionalized leaders of modern industrial unions and other protest groups who have a stake in non-violent protest (Baker, 2014).

The volatile 1998 Australian waterfront dispute revealed the relatively successful low-key and non-confrontational policing of that large-scale industrial conflict (Baker, 1999b). High profile, management-educated police leaders and union organizers endowed with public relations skills fostered communication, liaison and cooperation. Picketers were viewed as citizens on strike, not criminals. Although there have arguably been considerable successes with the dialogue and negotiated management approach adopted by police (the 1992 Associated Pulp and Paper Mill dispute at Burnie, the 1998 Australian waterfront dispute), there are signs that policing is attuned to not only communication but also to extensive paramilitary preparations (Baker, 1999a & 2005). The evidence indicates that police normally prepare for 'the worst case scenario', although they may also be prepared and willing to enter dialogue in order to prevent confrontation (P. A. J. Waddington, 2001). Some groups reject the authority of police and employ a diverse array of tactics; subsequently, police can employ a repertoire of tactical responses to maintain control dependant on police-protester history, forms of police knowledge, the local situation and modes of engagement (Gorringe & Rosie, 2008).

The intention is obviously to prevent violent clashes during industrial disputes. However, even if negotiations are breached and violence erupts, police need to have devised de-escalation tactics in order to curb excesses and the length of the confrontation. Inspector Sellenger played a significant role during the 1919 Fremantle 'battle of the barricades' in minimizing violence after Tommy Edwards received a fatal blow. In the frenzied atmosphere, Sellenger spoke and pacified the incensed crowd and appealed for the conciliatory intervention of both police and union leaders which led to the Premier withdrawing the 'volunteers' from the wharf. No such attempts at de-escalating confrontation occurred on the Northern coalfields after Norman Brown's shooting; the reverse happened with the 'basher gangs' besetting the mining communities. After ten people were killed three days prior to the Marikana massacre, the SAPS prepared for massive bloodshed; the plan for 16 August contained no de-escalation of violence component.

The question of the legitimacy or illegitimacy of a particular industrial protest may be vehemently contested by unions, employers, government and the media (della Porta, 1996, p. 65). Douglas (2004, pp. 26–29, 142) argues that Australian and state governments and the public have accepted a prima facie right to demonstrate as a legitimate form of expression. This operates successfully with predictable and planned protests, but is less appropriate for handling uncooperative or even confrontation-seeking crowds. The general expectation of aggressive employers is that police will react, if necessarily forcefully and repressively, in order to clear picket-lines (Finnane, 1994, pp. 13, 30; Baker, 1999a). Although most industrial disputes are settled by negotiation and court judgements, police alone clear obstructions or pickets from a plant or worksite. Court action pursued by employers to remove pickets only becomes effective when enforced by the police.

My suggestions for a 'best practice' approach of contemporary public order policing that stem from reflection on the deficiencies of the policing of the three historical case studies and the Marikana massacre, include the following:

- Effective policing of union activities has often occurred when the protest group has successfully 'self-policed' with police monitoring at a distance.
- Dialogue between police leaders and union organizers is desirable before, during and after the strike or lockout so that some understanding and contacts can be established and expanded.
- Clear communication and liaison are desirable between police leadership and union organizers whenever possible, with 'no

surprises'. Unionists, protesters and the public should be made aware of likely police action so that they can make informed decisions about their course of action (Her Majesty's Inspectorate of Constabulary, 2011, p. 39; Baker, 2014).
- When police endeavour to move picketers from a worksite, spatial factors need to be considered so that the picketers have the opportunity to be safely repositioned in another location.
- Police tactics need to be flexible and, whenever expedient, also transparent. Police tactics employed in the case studies examined in this book were dogmatic, inflexible, aggressive and prone to violence. As all industrial disputes are eventually resolved, police are well-advised, whenever possible, to hasten or act slowly in order to give the industrial structures and court processes enough time to adjudicate the dispute.
- If police coercion becomes inevitable, there should be focus not just on the methods of overcoming the resistance but also of establishing tactics for de-escalating the level of violent clashes.
- If coercion is required in a particular situation, such force should be appropriate and the minimum necessary.
- Appropriate public order training of police personnel of all levels, sadly lacking in 1920s Australia and at Marikana, is today identified as a key ingredient of successful monitoring and control of protest.
- Operational policing decisions need to be independent of the dictates of involved parties and devoid of any direct or indirect political interference or expectations of police to act aggressively. Employers and governments are entitled to criticize and make demands, but the important tenet is that police have the independence and flexibility to resist such pressures.
- Accountability of both police and protest actions must be thorough, appropriate and balanced. There was no accountability of those responsible for the deaths of Edwards, Whittaker and Brown. It is yet to be gauged how effective or otherwise the Farlam Commission of Inquiry will be in bringing violent offenders to justice.

Conclusion

The legacy and symbolism of violent police-unionist clashes endure. Tommy Edwards, Allan Whittaker and Norman Brown remain heroes in

Australian labour movement folklore. As a result of the brutal 16 August 2012 Marikana massacre at the Lonmin Mine, the South African Police Service's reputation is tarnished as a repressive and violent organization with roots in the apartheid regime's policing history of Sharpeville (1960) and Soweto (1976). Post-apartheid South Africa, evidenced by the Marikana massacre, is still struggling to prevent bloodshed in labour disputes. For police reform to be effective in the South African context, there is the need both to broaden the process of social change and assail social inequalities.

This book has explored a largely neglected aspect of Australian industrial relations and policing history. Fundamental criminological questions are raised in the case studies: 'What is the criminal act? Who is the criminal?' The book is an account of real people (police leaders, police on the street, union protesters, local community members) at specific places during decisive and volatile industrial epochs. It is a story well worth telling and one worthy of deliberation.

The book has documented the ill-fated policing of three fatalities at the hands of police during intense and bitter industrial disputes in early federated Australia. Fortunately, much has changed since those turbulent days – better educated and community-aware police leadership; union movement open to compromise and negotiation; working protocols between police and unions to prevent violence; a range of formal and informal accountability mechanisms; and institutionally, more robust and effective industrial conciliation and arbitration. However, police maintain the latent capacity to use force if deemed reasonable and appropriate to quell public disorder and to restore control and command.

Bibliography

Australian Broadcasting Commission, 774 Radio, 'PM', 1 May 2006.

Baker, D. (1999a). Avoiding 'War on the Wharves': Is the Non-confrontational Policing of Major Industrial Disputes 'Here to Stay'? *International Employment Relations Review*, 5(2), 39–62.

Baker, D. (1999b). Trade Unionism and the Policing Accord: Control and Self-Regulation of Picketing during the 1998 Maritime Dispute. *Labour and Industry*, 9(3), 123–144.

Baker, D. (2001a). The Fusion of Picketing, Policing and Public Order Theory within the Industrial Relations Context of the 1992 APPM Dispute at Burnie. *Australian Bulletin of Labour*, 27(1), 61–77.

Baker, D. (2001b). Barricades and Batons: A Historical Perspective of the Policing of Major Industrial Disorder in Australia. In M. Enders & B. Dupont (Eds), *Policing the Lucky Country* (pp.199–222). Annandale: Federation Press.

Baker, D. (2001c). Community Police Peacekeeping amidst Bitter and Divisive Industrial Confrontation. In R. Markey, (Ed.), *Labour and Community: Historical Essays* (pp. 174–200). Wollongong: University of Wollongong Press.

Baker, D. (2001d). Policing the 1873 Lothair mines dispute at Clunes. In P. Griffiths & R. Webb (Eds), *Work – Organisation – Struggle* (pp. 26–33). Canberra: Seventh National Labour History Conference, ANU.

Baker, D. (2002). *'You Dirty Bastards, Are You Fair Dinkum?'* Police and Union Confrontation on the Wharf. *New Zealand Journal of Industrial Relations*, 27(1), 33–47.

Baker, D. (2005). *Batons and Blockades: Policing Industrial Disputes in Australasia.* Melbourne: Circa.

Baker, D. (2007a). From Batons to Negotiated Management: The Transformation of Policing Industrial Disputes in Australia. *Policing: A Journal of Policy and Practice*, 1(4), 390–402.

Baker, D. (2007b). Policing, politics and civil rights: Analysis of the policing of protest against the 1999 Chinese President's visit to New Zealand. *Police Practice and Research: An International Journal*, 8(3), 219–238.

Baker, D. (2008). Paradoxes of policing and protest. *Policing, Intelligence and Counter Terrorism*, 3(2), 8–22.

Baker, D. (2012). Policing Contemporary Protests. In T. Prenzler (Ed.) *Policing and Security in Practice: Challenges and Achievement* (pp. 56–73). Basingstoke: Palgrave Macmillan.

Baker, D. (2014). Police and Protester Dialog: Safeguarding the peace or ritualistic sham? *International Journal of Comparative and Applied Criminal Justice*, 38(1), 83–104.

Beasley, M. (1996). *Wharfies: A History of the Waterside Workers' Federation of Australia.* Sydney: Halstead.

Blackmur, D. (1993). *Strikes: Causes, Conduct and Consequence.* Sydney: Federation Press.

Brecher, J. (1997). *Strike!* Cambridge (MA): South End Press.

Brewer, J., Guelke, A., Hume, I. & Wilford, R. (1988). *The Police, Public Order and the State.* Basingstoke: Macmillan Press.

Brogden, M. (1991). *On the Mersey Beat: Policing Liverpool between the Wars.* Oxford: Oxford University Press.

Brown, G. & Haldane, R. K. (1998). *Days of Violence: The 1923 Police Strike in Melbourne.* Ormond (Vic): Hybrid.

Budd, W. (1990). Australian Police in National Waterfront Riots 1928–1931. *Australian Police Journal*, 44(4): 137–144.

Bunbury, B. (2006). *Caught in Time: Talking Australian History.* Fremantle: Fremantle Arts Centre Press.

Burkhardt, P., Mbatha, A. & Cohen, M. (2013). Justice eludes South Africa year after Marikana massacre. 15 August. Bloomberg: accessed at http://www.bloomberg.com/news/print/2013-08-14/justice-eludes.

Cathcart, M. (1988). *Defending the National Tuckshop: Australia's Secret Army Intrigue of 1931.* Melbourne: McPhee.

Chinguno, C. (2014). Explaining violence in strikes. Presentation to the Marikana Commission of Inquiry, Violence in Industrial Relations seminar, University of Witwatersrand, Johannesburg, 16 April (pp. 6–25). Transcript accessed at http://www.marikanacomm.org.za/docs/20140416-SeminarPhase02-transcript.pdf.

City Press (14 April 2013). Demilitarising the police 'not the answer'.

City Press (2 April 2013). Police provoked Marikana miners – Bizos.

City Press (4 June 2013). Marikana operation done in humane manner – Phiyega.

City Press (6 June 2013). Marikana: Mpofu questions cops' lawlessness.

Cohen, R. (2013). The Marikana tragedy: South Africa's social contract with its working poor breaks down. *Inroads: A Journal of Opinion*, 32, 108–112.

Collins, R. (2008). *Violence: A Micro-sociological Theory*. Princeton (NJ): Princeton University Press.

Comerford, J. (2006). *Lockout*. Sydney: CFMEU Mining and Industry print.

Crawford, D. J. (1987). *An Outline of Commonwealth Policing 1911–1987*. Unpublished, Australian Federal Police.

Crothers, L. & Ana P. (2013). Police deny responsibilities for shooting civilians. *Cambodian Daily*, 14 November.

Dawson, W. (Interview, 1978). Recalling Rothbury, 1929. *Common Cause* (*Miners' Federation Journal*), 27 September, p. 2.

Deery, P. (1995). Chifley, the Army and the 1949 Coal Strike. *Labour History*, 68, 80–92.

de Garis, B. (1966). An Incident at Fremantle. *Labour History*, 10, 32–37.

della Porta, D. & Reiter, H. (Eds) (1998). *Policing Protest: The Control of Mass Demonstrations in Western Democracies*. Minneapolis: University of Minnesota Press.

della Porta, D., Peterson A. & Reiter H. (2006). *The Policing of Transnational Protest*. Aldershot: Ashgate.

DeMichele, M. (2008). Policing Protest Events: The Great Strike of 1877 and WTO Protests of 1999. *American Journal of Criminal Justice*, 33, 1–18.

Dixon, B. (2013). Waiting for Farlam: Marikana, social inequality and the relative autonomy of the police. *South African Crime Quarterly*, 56, 5–11.

Dixson, M. (1983). Stubborn Resistance: the Northern New South Wales Miners' Lockout of 1929–1930. In D. J. Murphy (Ed.), *The Big Strikes:*

Queensland 1889–1965 (pp. 136–141). St. Lucia: Queensland University Press.

Douglas, R. (2004). *Dealing with Demonstrations: The Law of Public Protest and its Enforcement*. Annandale: Federation Press.

Earl, J., Soule, S. & McCarthy, J. (2003). Protest under Fire? Explaining the Policing of Protest. *American Sociological Review*, 68(4), 581–606.

Earl, J. (2003). Tanks, tear gas, and taxes: Toward a theory of movement repression. *Sociological Theory*, 21(1), 44–68.

Earl, J. & Soule, S. (2006). Seeing blue: A police-centered explanation of protest policing. *Mobilization: An International Journal*, 11(2), 145–164.

Earl, J. (2006). Introduction: Repression and the social control of protest. *Mobilization: An International Journal*, 11(2), 129–143.

Ericson, R. & Doyle, A. (1999). Globalization and the policing of protest: the case of APEC 1997. *British Journal of Sociology*, 50(4), 589–608.

Evans, R. (2005). William John MacKay and the New South Wales police force, 1910–1948: a study of police power. PhD thesis, School of Political and Social Science, Monash University.

Evans, R. (2012). 'Murderous Coppers'; Police, industrial disputes and the 1929 Rothbury shootings. *History Victoria*, 9(1), pp. 176–200.

Evans, S. (2013). Marikana: Mpembe's thin blue line failed miners. *Mail & Guardian*, 19 June.

Evans, S. (2014). Marikana: 'Fall guy' cop cuts a lonely figure. *Mail & Guardian*, 28 March.

Falanga, G. (2014a). Deep flaws in police unit exposed at Marikana inquiry. *Mail & Guardian*, 11 April.

Falanga, G. (2014b). Marikana: North West cop sobs during cross-examination. *Mail & Guardian*, 24 April.

Falanga, G. (2014c). State gets 'off the hook' on Marikana. *Mail & Guardian*, 23 May.

Falanga, G. (2014d). 'Toxic' Lonmin-police collusion blamed for Marikana massacre. *Mail & Guardian*, 30 July.

Falanga, G. (2014e). Mr X insists SAPS, Lonmin are innocent. *Mail & Guardian*, 22 July.

Fernandez, L. (2008). *Policing Dissent: Social Control and the Anti-Globalization Movement*. New Brunswick: Rutgers University Press.

Finnane, M. (1994). *Police and Government: Histories of Policing in Australia.* Melbourne: Oxford University Press.

Frankel, P. (2001). *An ordinary atrocity: Sharpeville and its massacre.* New Haven: Yale.

Garritty, P. (2010). When police shot Anzacs. *Green-Left Weekly*, 858, October 23.

Geary, R. (1985). *Policing Industrial Disputes.* London: Cambridge University Press.

Gillham, P. & Noakes, J. (2007). 'More than a March in a Circle': Transgressive protests and the limits of negotiated management. *Mobilization: An International Quarterly*, 12(4), 341–357.

Goko, C. (2013). Police accused of lying to Marikana commission. *Business Day Live*, 20 September.

Gollan, R. (1963). *The Coalminers of New South Wales: A History of the Union, 1860–1960.* Carlton: Melbourne University Press.

Gorringe, H. & Rosie, M. (2008). It is a long way to Auchterarder! 'Negotiated management' and mismanagement in the policing of G8 protests. *British Journal of Sociology*, 59(2), 187–205.

Gorringe, H., Rosie, M., Waddington, D., & Kominou, M. (2012). Facilitating ineffective protest? The policing of the 2009 Edinburgh NATO protests. *Policing and Society: An International Journal of Research and Policy*, 22(2), 115–132.

Govender, D. (2013). Review of I. Kinnes' book, *Public order policing in South Africa: Capacity, constraints and capabilities.* Pinelands (South Africa): Open Society Federation for South Africa. Review located in the *South African Journal of Criminology*, 26(2), 170–172.

Grant, D. & Wallace, M. (1991). Why do strikes turn violent? *American Journal of Sociology*, 96(5): 1117–1150.

Griffiths, B. (1989). *Wharfies: A Celebration of 100 Years on the Fremantle Waterfront 1889–1989.* West Perth: Platypus.

Haldane, R. K. (1995). *The People's Force: A History of the Victoria Police.* Carlton: Melbourne University Press.

Hall, A. & de Lint, W. (2003). Policing labour in Canada. *Policing and Society*, 13(3), 219–234.

Hall, A. & de Lint, W. (2004). Making the pickets responsible: Policing labour at a distance in Windsor, Ontario. In S. N. Nancoo (Ed.), *Contemporary Issues in Canadian Policing* (pp. 337–375). Mississauga: Canadian Educators Press.

Hawke, J. (1999). Seeds sown for Rothbury's riot. *Common Cause*, 16 December.

Her Majesty's Inspectorate of Constabulary. (2011). An overview and review of progress against the recommendations of *Adapting to Protest and Nurturing the British Model of Policing*. London: HMIC.

Hetherington, (1973). *Blamey: Controversial Soldier*. Canberra: Australian War Memorial.

Hoare, Q. & South, G. (1971, Translators and Eds). Selections from the Prison Notebooks of Antonio Gramsci. London: Lawrence and Wishart.

Hoggett, T. & Stott, C. (2010). The role of crowd theory in determining the use of force in public order policing. *Policing and Society: An International Journal of Research and Policy*, 20(2): 223–236.

Hopper, P. (1975). The 1919 Fremantle Lumpers' Strike. Unpublished BA Hons thesis, Perth, University of Western Australia.

Horner, D. (1998). *Blamey: The Commander-in-Chief*. Sydney: Allen and Unwin.

Hutchinson, D. (2006). 'Bloody Sunday' revisited. Unpublished, final draft. Fremantle City Library.

Ichikowitz, I. (2012). Modernising police makes economic sense. *New African*, 552, 34–35, November.

Jefferson, T. 1990. *The Case against Paramilitary Policing*. Milton Keynes: Open University Press.

Joint Committee on Human Rights. (2009). Demonstrating respect for rights? A human rights approach to policing protest. Seventh Report of Session, HL Paper 47–1, published 23 March, London.

Kraska, P. & Kappeler, V. (1997). Militarizing American Police: The Rise and Normalization of Paramilitary Units. *Social Problems*, 44(1): 1–18.

Kraska, P. & Kappeler, V. (2005). Militarizing American Police: The Rise and Normalization of Paramilitary Units. In V. Kappeler (Ed.) *The Police and Society: Touchstone Readings* (pp. 463–480). Prospect Heights: Waveland Press.

Kratcoski, P. Verma, A. & Das, D. (2001). Policing of public order: a world perspective. *Police Practice and Research: An International Journal*, 2(1–2):109–143.

Kumara, S. (2013). Protests intensify in Bangladesh after police kill two garment workers. World Socialist website, 20 November.

Ledwaba, L. (2013a). Police book contradicts Marikana 'self-defence' argument. *City Press*, 21 April.

Ledwaba, L. (2013b). Marikana plan was 110% effective. *Sowetan*, 3 October, p. 2.

Lipes, J. (2013, Translator). Woman shot dead by Cambodian Police in protest clampdown. *Cambodian Daily*, 12 November.

Lockwood, R. (1990). *Ship to Shore: A History of Melbourne's Waterfront and its Union Struggles*. Sydney: Hale and Iremonger.

Lovell, J. (2009). *Crimes of Dissent: Civil Disobedience, Criminal Justice and the Politics of Conscience*. New York: New York University Press.

Lowenstein, W. & Hills, T. (1982). *Under the Hook: Melbourne Waterside Workers Remember: 1900–1980*. Prahran: Bookworkers Press.

Mail & Guardian (2014 editorial). Lie, deny, then blame others. 28 March.

Mail & Guardian (2013). Marikana deaths caused by individuals, not plan, say police. 24 October.

Malala, J. (2013). No end in sight for police brutality in South Africa. *The Guardian*, 22 February.

Marinovich, G. (2012). The murder fields of Marikana. The cold murder fields of Marikana. *Daily Maverick*, 30 August.

Marinovich, G. (2013). Marikana: Policeman accuses fellow officer of killing wounded miner. *Daily Maverick*, 21 March.

Maromo, J. (2013). Marikana commission: strikers used *muti*, believed they were invincible. *Mail & Guardian*, 26 November.

Marx, G. (1998). Some Reflections on the Democratic Policing of Demonstrations. In D. della Porta & H. Reiter, *Policing Protest: The Control of Mass Demonstrations in Western Democracies* (pp. 253–270). Minneapolis: University of Minnesota Press.

McCallum, D. F. *People Places and Politics*. Unpublished Memoirs of Donald Feres McCallum, 1973, Chapter 4 (personal papers), JCPML00905/1, John Curtin Prime Ministerial Library, Curtin University, Perth, Western Australia.

McClenaghan, M. (2013). Church seeks answers over South African mine massacre. *The Observer*, 24 November.

McConville, C. (1983). 1888 – the Policeman's Lot (1988). In *Australia 1988*, no.11, May: 78–87.

McCulloch, J. (2001). *Blue Army: Paramilitary Policing in Australia*. Carlton: Melbourne University Press.

McPhail, C., Schweingruber, D. & McCarthy, J. (1998). Policing Protest in the United States: 1960–1995. In D. della Porta & H. Reiter

(Eds), *Policing Protest: The Control of Mass Demonstrations in Western Democracies* (pp. 49–69). University of Minnesota Press.
Miller, S., Blackler, J. & Alexandra, A. (1997). *Police Ethics*. Sydney: Allen and Unwin.
Moore, A. (1987). Policing enemies of the state. In Finnane. M. (Ed.), *Policing in Australia: Historical Perspectives* (pp.114–142). Melbourne: Oxford University Press.
Murphy, D. J. (1975). *T. J. Ryan: A Political Biography*. St. Lucia: University of Queensland Press.
Nare, S. (2014a). Mpofu goes for Calitz. *Daily Sun*, 22 January, p. 2.
Nare, S. (2014b). Police versions clash. *Daily Sun*, 24 January, p. 4.
Newham, G. (2014). How can the South African Police Service prevent another Marikana? Presentation to the Marikana Commission of Inquiry, Violence in Industrial Relations seminar, University of Witwatersrand, Johannesburg, 16 April, pp. 45–68. Transcript accessed at http://www.marikanacomm.org.za/docs/20140416-SeminarPhase02-transcript.pdf.
News24. (12 September 2013). Government taking sides – Marikana widow. Accessed at http:/www.news24.com/.
Nhlabath, H. (2013a). Police not on the same wavelength. *Sowetan*, 26 April, p. 4.
Nhlabath, H. (2013b). Witness admits to police blunder in Marikana massacre. *Sowetan Live*, 30 April. Accessed at http://www.sowetanlive.co.za/news./2013/04/30/witness.
Nyland, C. & Svensen, S. (1995). The Battle of Bombo – Besetting Laws and the Right to Picket in New South Wales. *Australian Journal of Labour Law*, 8(3), 177–202.
Oliver, B. (1990). Disputes, Diggers and Disillusionment: Social and Industrial Unrest in Perth and Kalgoorlie 1918–1924. In J. Gregory (Ed.), *Studies in Western Australian History XI: Western Australia between the Wars, 1919–1939* (pp. 19–28). Perth: University of Western Australia.
Oliver, B. (1995). *War and Peace in Western Australia: The social and political impact of the Great War, 1914–1926*. Nedlands: University of Western Australia.
Oliver, B. (2003). *Unity is Strength: A History of the Australian Labour Party and the Trades and Labour Council in Western Australia, 1899–1999*. Perth: API Network.

O'Malley, P. (1983). *Law, Capitalism and Democracy*. London: Allen and Unwin.

Patel, K. (2013). The Marikana Commission, and skewed access to justice. *Daily Maverick*, 15 August.

Paton, C. (2013). Stage set for inquiry as battle between state and the people. *Business Day Live*, 15 August. Accessed at http://bdlive.co.za/opinion/2013/08/15/stage-set-for-inquiry.

Petrus, T. (2014). Enemies of the People: Reflections on the South African Police Service (SAPS) as a Symbol of Repression and Oppression Post-1994. *International Journal of Humanities and Social Science*, 4(2), 68–79.

Polygreen, L. (2012). Strike by armed miners in South Africa provokes a fatal police response. *New York Times*, 17 August, p. A8.

Ramutsindela, M. (2013). Violent political and economic geographies of mining. *Political Geography*, 33, A1–A2.

Reicher, S. (2011). From crisis to opportunity: New crowd psychology and public order policing principles. In T. Madensen & J. Knutsson (Eds), *Preventing Crowd Violence* (pp. 7–23). London: Lynne Rienner.

Reiner, R. (2000). *The Politics of the Police*. Oxford: Oxford University Press.

Saba, A. (2013). Change of plan for police hours before Marikana massacre. *City Press*, 21 June.

SABC (2013a). Police expert slates Marikana police approach. 31 October.

SABC (2013b). I didn't know miners were dead, cop tells Marikana Commission. 25 November.

Sarre, R. (2001). The Policing of Public Order in Australia. *Police Practice and Research: An International Journal*, 2(1–2), 53–70.

Satgar, V. (2012). Beyond Marikana: the post-Apartheid South African State. *Africa Spectrum*, 47(2–3), 53–59.

Shelembe, N. (2014). South Africa: Strikers Kill Police during Confrontation. South African Press Association, 24 June. Accessed at http://allafrica.com/stories/201406241566.html.

Shenker, J. (2014). After the massacre: Life in South Africa's mining belt. *The Guardian* (UK), 16 August.

Sheridan, T. (1994). Australian Wharfies 1943–1967: Casual attitudes, militant leadership and workplace change. *The Journal of Industrial Relations*, 36(2), 258–284.

Silvester, J. & Rule, P. (2010). Truth was first casualty of 1928 war on the waterfront. *Sydney Morning Herald*, 6 November.
Skolnick, J. (1971). *The Politics of Protest*. New York: Ballantine.
Smith, D. (2013). Nearly 1500 South African police exposed as convicted criminals. *The Guardian*, 16 August.
Smith, M. (2013). The Marikana Massacre and Lessons for the Left. *Irish Marxist Review*, 2(5), 53–64.
Sosibo, K. (2013). Marikana's tangled web unravels. *Mail & Guardian*, 25 October.
Sosibo, K. (2014). Marikana commission: 'Unknown' value of mystery Mr X. *Mail & Guardian*, 4 April.
Taft, J. & Ross, P. (1979). American Labor Violence: Its Causes, Character and Outcome. In H. D. Graham & E. R. Gurr, (Eds), *Violence in America: Historical and Comparative Perspectives* (vol.1, pp. 187–241). California: Sage Publications.
Terry Laidler, 'drive' radio program, ABC 3LO, 17 March 1999.
The Marikana Commission of Inquiry (2012–2014). Available: http://www.marikanacomm.org.za.
The Star (2013). Police chief triggers gasps of disbelief. 18 April.
Thiebolt, A. & Haggard, T. R. (1983). *Union Violence: The Record and the Response by Courts, Legislatures and the NLRB*. Industrial Relations Research Unit, University of Pennsylvania.
Tobias, J. (1977). The British Colonial Police. In P. J. Stead (Ed.), *Pioneers in Policing* (pp. 241–261). New Jersey: McGraw-Hill.
Tolsi, N. & Evans, S. (2013). New Marikana footage points finger at police. *Mail & Guardian*, 21 October.
Turner, I. (1976). *In Union is Strength: a history of trade unions in Australia, 1788–1978*. Melbourne: Thomas Nelson.
Turner, J. (2013). Do the English and South African Criminal Justice Systems share a 'Common Purpose'? *African Journal of International and Comparative Law*, 21 (2), 295–300.
Twala, C. (2012). The Marikana Massacre: A Historical Overview of the Labour Unrest in the Mining sector in South Africa. *Southern African Peace and Security Studies*. 1(2), 61–67.
Uglow, S. (1988). *Policing Liberal Society*. Oxford: Oxford University Press.
Van der Spuy, E. & Shearing, C. (2014). Curbing the Killing Fields: Making South Africa Safer. *The Annals of the American Academy of Political and Social Science*. 652, 186–205.

Van Graan, M. (2013). The Spear and the Marikana massacre: mirroring the decline of South African democracy. *African Arts*, 46(2), 1–5.

Victorian Parliamentary Debates (Legislative Assembly), 1928, vols. 177 & 178.

Vitale, A. (2007). The command and control and Miami models at the 2004 Republican National Convention: New forms of policing protests. *Mobilization: An International Quarterly*, 12(4), 403–415.

Waddington, D. (1992). *Contemporary Issues in Public Disorder: A comparative and historical approach*. London: Routledge.

Waddington, D. (2007). *Policing Public Disorder: Theory and Practice*. Devon: Willan.

Waddington, D., Jones, K. & Critcher, C. (1989). *Flashpoints: Studies in Public Disorder*. London: Routledge.

Waddington, P. A. J. (1994). *Liberty and Order: Public Order Policing in a Capital City*. London: UCL Press.

Waddington, P. A. J. (1999). *Policing Citizens: authority and rights*. London: UCL Press.

Waddington, P. A. J. (2001). Negotiating and Defining 'Public Order'. *Police Practice and Research: An International Journal*, 2(1–2), 3–14.

Waddington, P. A. J. (2007). Public order: Then and now. In A. Henry & D. Smith (Eds), *Transformations of Policing* (pp. 113–140). Aldershot: Ashgate.

Webb, B. (1994). *A History of William Charles Sellenger*. Typescript monograph: Fremantle Local History Library.

Webster, E. (2014). Strike Violence: an alternative avenue. Presentation to the Marikana Commission of Inquiry, Violence in Industrial Relations seminar, University of Witwatersrand, Johannesburg, 16 April (pp. 26–44). Transcript accessed at http://www.marikanacomm.org.za/docs/20140416-SeminarPhase02-transcript.pdf.

Weinberger, B. (1991). *Keeping the Peace? Policing strikes in Britain, 1906–1926*. Oxford: Berg.

White, R. & Perrone, S. (2005). *Crime and Social Control*. Carlton: Melbourne University Press.

Williams, C. (2007). Tough men, hard times policing the depression. *Police News* (NSW), April, pp. 20, 22.

Williams, J. (1976). *The First Furrow*. Willagree: Lone Hand Press.

Willis, A. (2001). Public order policing in the UK: a fading star? *Police Practice and Research: An International Journal*, 2(1–2), 15–26.

Wright, R. (1992). *A People's Counsel: A History of the Parliament of Victoria*. Melbourne: Oxford University Press.

Xaba, V. (2014). Charge highest cops with murder. *Sowetan*, 24 January, p. 6.

Archival materials

Western Australia Police Department Files of correspondence and internal police reports 1918–1919 (hereafter cited as PDF), State Records Office of WA [SROWA] Accession no 430, File 4092/1918 and File 2396/1919 (as cited in Chapter 4).
Commissioner of Police to Colonial Secretary, 4 March & 16 April 1918, PDF 4092/1918.
Inspector Sellenger to Commissioner of Police, 16 & 17 November 1918, PDF 4092/1918.
Inspector Mann to Commissioner of Police, 9 May 1919, PDF 2396/1919.
Commissioner of Police to Colonial Secretary, 16 April 1919, PDF 2396/1919; administration PDF 2400/1919.
Commissioner of Police's telegrams to Inspectors Houlahan (14 April), Mitchell (14 April) and Walsh (15 April), PDF 2400/1919.
Commissioner of Police to Sellenger, 12 May 1919, PDF 2396/1919.
Chief Inspector McKenna to Commissioner of Police, 15 April 1919; 9 & 13 May 1919, PDF 2396/1919.
Sellenger to Commissioner of Police, 15 April 1919; 8, 10, 12 & 16 May 1919, PDF 2396/1919.
Sergeant Simpson and Constable Baker, 7 May 1919, to Sellenger, forwarded to Commissioner of Police, 8 May 1919, PDF 2936/1919.
Sergeant Johnston to Inspector O'Halloran, 15 May 1919, PDF 2396/1919.
Constable Wilson to Chief Inspector McKenna (forwarded to Commissioner Connell), 12 May 1919, PDF 2396/1919.

Newspapers

Cessnock Eagle: 17, 18, 20 & 24 December 1929; 14 & 17 January 1930; 11, 14 & 18 February 1930.
Daily Mail, 25 November 2013.
Daily News, 29 & 30 May 1919, 5 June 1919.
Daily Telegraph Pictorial, 17 December 1929.
Fremantle Times, 9 & 16 May 1919; 13 June 1919.

Kurri Kurri Times: 12 & 19 December 1929; 16 January 1930.
Labor Daily: 10, 11, 14, 16, 20, 22 & 25 January 1930; 1 November 1930.
Maitland Daily Mercury: 6, 13 & 16 January 1930; 11–13 & 18 February 1930; 16 May 1930.
Newcastle Morning Herald & Miners' Advocate: 16, 17, 18, 20 & 21 December 1929; 11, 16, 21 & 22 January 1930; 14, 15 & 18 February 1930; 12 December 1930.
Smith's Weekly, 21 December 1929; 25 January 1930.
Sunday Times, 11 May 1919.
Sydney Morning Herald, 14, 17, 18 & 23 December 1929; 16 & 20 January 1930.
The Age, 11 December 1873; 3 & 5 November 1928.
The Labour Call, 8 November 1928, vol. xxii, no.1146.
West Australian, 3, 6, 9, 29, 30 & 31 May 1919; 6 June 1919.
Westralian Worker, 25 April 1919; 9 May 1919.

Index

African National Congress, 17, 18, 20, 22, 31
agents provocateurs, 54
ALF Disputes Committee, 46
Argyle, Stanley, 60
Association of Chief Police Officers, 9
Association of Mineworkers and Construction Union (AMCU), 20, 26
Australian Seamen's Union, 54

Bangladesh, 13–14
Bavin state government, 67–69, 73
Beattie, Alexander, 72–73, 75–78
Beeby, George, Justice, 54, 72
'best practice' policing, 88–92
Bizos, George, 28
Blamey, Thomas, 57–64, 88
'Bloody Sunday', 39–51
Bombings, 11, 55
Botes, Dirk, 31
Brecher, Jeremy, 13
Brogden, Michael, 5
Brown, Edward, 43, 45, 48, 50
Brown, Norman, 6, 66–67, 71, 74, 79–83, 91–92

Calitz, Adriaan, 27, 29
Cambodian riot police, 14
Childs, Walter, 71–72
Citizens' Defence Brigade, 54
Colebatch, Hal, 42, 48, 50
Comerford, Jim, 68, 71–72, 76
Commonwealth Peace Officers, 54
Communication, 3, 6–8, 16, 20, 29, 34, 39, 51, 65, 84–91
communist hysteria, 4, 38, 54, 80, 87
Communists, 54, 62, 80, 82
Comrie, Neil, 13
conciliation and arbitration, 20, 38, 54, 69, 87, 93
Connell, Robert, 41, 43–48
Coronial inquests, 6, 36, 47–48, 61–62, 66, 80, 82, 86
   Clancy, J. (Mailtland), 81–82
   Curtis, W. J. (Maitland), 81–82
   Dowley, E. P. (Fremantle), 47
   Reed, D. W. (Maitland District Coroner), 80

Dawson, Wal, 70, 73
Della Porta, Donnatella and Reiter, Herbert, 4, 7, 32
Desai, Rehad, 30
Detheridge Royal Commission, 38, 40
Dimboola, 36, 41

Edwards, Tommy, 6, 36, 39, 43, 46–51, 67, 82–83, 91–92
Ericson, Richard and Doyle, Aaron, 8

108 Index

escalated force, 1, 7
Evans, Richard, 75

Farlam Commission of Inquiry, 16, 26–34, 92
fatalities, 1, 13, 15, 17, 35, 59, 83, 85, 86, 93
'flying squad', 68, 77–78, 83
force, 1–4, 7, 9, 11–19, 22–25
  minimum force, 3, 28
Fremantle wharf, 36, 38, 40, 42, 48

Gollan, Robin, 79
Graham, Paul, 25
Gramsci, Antonio, 2
Grant, D. S. and Wallace, M., 63

Haldane, Robert, 59, 63
Hall, A. and de Lint, W., 8
Hendrickx, Eddie, 27
Hogan, E. J., 54–55, 58, 60

industrial disputes, 3, 5, 14–17, 35, 37, 39, 46–47, 50, 52, 62, 67–68, 83, 86, 90–93
  Associated Pulp and Paper Mill dispute (1992), 90
  Australian waterfront dispute (1998), 7, 13, 50, 64, 90
  Brisbane general strike (1912), 53
  Clunes riot (1873), 38, 40
  coal strike (1949), 53
  General strike (1917), 38
  Melbourne police strike (1923), 55
  Sydney timber strike (1929), 67–68

Labor Call, 56–59
Lang, Jack, 74, 83
Lessons for policing, 12, 8, 15, 17, 35, 85–93
Lonmin mining company, 19–20, 23, 26–31, 33, 93
lumpers, 38–50

MacKay, William, 68, 75, 77–78, 83
Mann, Harry, 39, 42, 44, 46, 48

Marikana massacre, 14, 16–35, 85, 86, 91, 93
Marikana strike, 20, 87
Maritime Union of Australia, 65
Mbombo, Zukiswa, 23, 27, 29, 31
McCallum, Alex, 41–46, 48
mining communities (northern NSW), 66, 73, 77–79, 91
Morris, James, 56, 61
Mossop (Sub-Inspector), 52, 56–58, 60
Mpembe, William, 27, 29
Mpofu, Dali, 27, 31
Mr X, 30

Nagel, Jim, 59
National Union of Miners (NUM), 20–21, 26, 31
negotiated management, 1, 7–8, 10, 89–90
Newham, Gareth, 31–32
Northern NSW coalfields, 66–67, 77, 89

'outside' police, 66–69, 76–77, 79, 83, 86, 88

Phiyega, Rhia, 23, 28, 29, 31
picketing/picket-lines/lockouts, 1, 5, 8, 12–15, 17, 36, 38–41, 50, 53, 56, 63–64, 68–72, 76–77, 85, 87–92
  peaceful and passive, 3
Platinum mines, 14, 19, 26, 33
police, *passim*
  accountability, 6, 13, 15, 35, 37, 73, 85–88, 92–93
  archives, 39
  control and command, 11, 93
  crowd interaction and management, 15, 22, 25, 35
  discretion, 3, 25, 47, 72
  independence and impartiality, 2, 25, 64, 65, 92
  internal investigations, 6, 14, 34, 88
  legitimacy, 2–3, 18, 20, 89–91
  mandate, 2, 34, 37, 64, 86
  mind-set, 83
  original authority, 24

police, *passim* – continued
  paramilitary units, 10
  partisan agents, 53
  protection of strike-breaking labour, 38, 40, 49, 54, 56, 69
  public order training and planning, 6, 25, 87–88, 92
  reputation, 16, 34, 56, 61, 93
  shootings, 6, 14, 17, 24, 27, 52, 56–61, 66, 71, 73, 74
  social control, 3
  tactics, 2, 5, 7, 11, 25–26, 58, 75, 80, 83, 86–87, 90–92
  traditional police response, 37–38
  use of baton, 4, 14, 36, 48–50, 55–59, 62, 70, 72–73, 76–78, 83
  video surveillance, 10, 89
'police'
  'policing at a distance', 8
Port Adelaide waterfront, 62
Port Melbourne, 52, 56–65, 72, 83, 89
Port Phillip Stevedores' Association, 55, 57, 60
Potchefstroom, 27
Prince's Pier, Port Melbourne, 56–60
protests
  anti-globalization, 8, 9, 11
  APEC, Sydney (2007), 11
  Free Tibet, 9
  Genoa and Gothenburg (2001), 11
  Melbourne's G20 protest (2006), 10
  single-issue, 9
public order literature, 7–12
public order policing, 2, 6, 9, 15, 22, 25, 29, 34, 57, 91
  worst-case scenarios, 10, 11, 17, 90

Ramaphosa, Cyril, 31
Renton, William, 41–43, 48
rock drill operators, 19–21
Rothbury mine, 68, 70
Rothbury riot, 66–75, 80
Royal Canadian Mounted Police, 8

Scott, Duncan, 24, 25, 29, 30

Scullin, James, 77
Sellenger, William, 39–50, 88, 91
Shabangu, Susan, 18
Sharpeville massacre, 1960, 16–17, 33, 93
Shelley, Joseph, 80
Sokhum, Eng, 14
South African Police (SAP), 17, 18
South African Police Service (SAPS), 16, 17–19, 21–27, 30, 32–34, 87–88, 91
  history and legacy, 18
  remilitarization, 18
  Tactical Response Team, 30
Soweto (1976), 93
strategic incapacitation, 1, 11

Taft, Philip and Ross, Philip, 12

U.S.A., 12
Uglow, Steve, 57
union organizers, 3, 8, 10, 50, 85, 88, 90
unionists, 5, 4, 37, 49–50, 54–58, 60, 67–69, 73, 76–77, 82, 86–89, 92
Unlawful Assembly Act (NSW), 68

Vermaak, Salmon, 29
Victoria Police Force, 10, 13, 55–56, 61, 65
Vietnam War moratoriums, 6
Vincent, Frank, Justice, 61
violence, *passim*
  'volunteer', 38, 42, 44–45, 55–56, 58, 69–71, 74, 81, 91

Waddington, David, 7, 28
Waddington, P. A. J., 3, 7, 28
Waterside Workers' Federation, 54
Weaver, Reginald, 68–71, 73–75
White Army (Victoria), 63
Whittaker, Allan, 6, 52, 59–63, 67, 82, 83, 92
'wildcat' strikers, 4, 11, 14, 16, 19, 20, 22, 32–33

Zuma, Jacob, 18, 20, 23, 26

CPSIA information can be obtained at www.ICGtesting.com
Printed in the USA
LVOW11*1825040315

429280LV00006B/124/P